DATE DUE			
JAN 26 '04			
AUG 11 '04			
MAY 05 '06			
MR 01 '16			
MY 17 '16			
AP 04 '18			

Cranes

CRANES

The Noblest Flyers

In Natural History & Cultural Lore

ALICE LINDSAY PRICE

La Alameda Press   Albuquerque

Grateful acknowledgment is made to the following
for permission to include their work:
photograph of ultralights leading Cranes
(courtesy of Operation Migration)
Whooping Crane head by Mark Catesby
(courtesy of Gilcrease Museum)
"Sloan Crane" by John White
(courtesy of The British Museum)
photograph of Aldo Leopold
(courtesy of the Aldo Leopold Foundation, Baraboo, WI)
painting of the World's Cranes
(David Rankin / courtesy of The International Crane Foundation)
Whooping & Sandhill Crane distribution maps
(courtesy of Marion Loucks Design)

Cover photograph: *Cranes at Bosque del Apache*
Copyright © 2001 by Dennis Welker

Various illustrations and photographs
used throughout the book are by the author,
unless otherwise noted.

ISBN: 1-888809-24-8

Library of Congress Card Number: 2001 132056

La Alameda Press
9636 Guadalupe Trail NW
Albuquerque, New Mexico 87114

5/03   12853

Table of Contents

Preface

"The noblest thing that flies," which Ernest Thompson Seton wrote upon seeing Whooping Cranes, is the inspiration for the title of this book. Some readers might protest at the spelling "flyers" and hold on tightly to the equally valid "fliers." However, I assure you that "flyers" was chosen to stress that sense of animation we all feel when seeing Cranes speeding aloft across the American skies.

When beginning research on this story of the two North American birds, the Sandhill and Whooping Cranes and their survival into the twenty-first century, I came across a passage by the great Walden Pond naturalist, Henry David Thoreau. I copied the passage by hand and then pinned it above my computer.

In his journal entry of February 16,1860, Thoreau establishes an enduring principle. Concerned about the state of natural history in his day he writes,"I think that the most important requisite in describing an animal is to be sure and give its character and spirit, for in that you have, without error the sum and effect of all its parts, known and un-known. You must show what it is to man. Surely the most important part of an animal is its anima, the vital spirit, on which is based its character in all its peculiarities which most concerns us. . . . A history of animal nature must be animated."

Thoreau's words have always been before me as a guide. Consequently,to write a natural history so that the Sandhills and Whooping Cranes are alive to you in all their "vital spirit" is my aim in these pages. And I hope, if you have not done so already, you will go to those places where it is possible to observe them for yourself.

To show what the Cranes are to human observers, I have incorporated the cultural lore of literature, myth and story, within their natural histories. The energies within the lore of birds are real, extending from a deep past to us. Sometimes, unaware that we are doing so, we may grasp certain essential truths in ourselves and in our relation to animals.

An entire cultural matrix has been created by humans telling stories of birds. Clearly, the birds' deft escape from the bonds of earth as they fly toward heaven has moved us earthlings since time before time. As you will see in pages to come, associations with the Crane as a messenger bird of healing, longevity and immortality are signs encircling the globe. These positive human connections with the Crane abound in artifact and myth of Europe and Africa, in North America's native story and ceremony, and in Asia's religious and secular traditions. Thus we realize as poet William Stafford does when "Watching Sandhill Cranes" that "they are not quite our own, not quite the world's."

That we may yet feel this unworldly sense of awe when looking up to see Cranes overhead is owed to the life-scientists and avian scholars, particularly of the last century and the present one. Starting in the late 1940s, only a few scientists began the battle for the Cranes' survival. The Whooping Cranes' numbers had fallen to a mere sixteen birds, only something as ephemeral as a few feathers seemed to come between them and extinction. The Sandhills, although always more populous than the Whoopers, were also beginning to slip away from us, their numbers falling. This was a situation only recognized by a few such as Aldo Leopold of "land ethic" fame who counted their thinning numbers in his own Wisconsin skies.

There are no doubt other heroes unknown to me in this struggle to save the Cranes, but I have focused on the works of those active in field and wetland—mid-century and today—the scientists and also the "thousand-hour-volunteer" whom I met at Aransas Wildlife Refuge. All of them, scientist or volunteer, epitomize the great effort made in the Crane's behalf. For writers who have chronicled the Crane's story earlier, I have turned to Robin Doughty, Barbara Katz, Paul Johnsgard, Faith McNulty and Jerome J. Pratt.

My thanks to scientists close to Cranes, George Archibald and Roderick Drewien, who looked over portions of this work, but any wandering off-course would be entirely my own. Also thanks to Delores "Dee" Isted, consummate birder, who gave me some pointers, and also Nyla and Randy Woody, leaders of the Audubon Society tour to Bosque del Apache.

I am grateful to Dr. Spencer Weersing, a Michigan dentist and friend of fellow dentist Dr. Lawrence Walkinshaw. Dr. Weersing lent me Walkinshaw's remarkable books on Cranes.

For other lore, I have consulted those in differing fields such as James B. Thayer, geologist; Garrick Bailey, anthropologist; Mary Yeakey, Latin scholar and translator; Ivy Dempsey, poet; Caroline Swinson, librarian, and, of course my guide to the waterworld of birds, Russell Studebaker, horticulturist and garden writer.

To all these, this work is dedicated, also to include those of you who take the time to find those silent spaces and look up to watch the birds.

Language of the
Sandhill Crane

Then some day here come the cranes
planing in from cloud or mist — sharp,
lonely spears awkwardly graceful.
They reach for the land; they stalk
the ploughed fields, not letting us near,
not quite our own, not quite the world's.

WILLIAM STAFFORD
"Watching Sandhill Cranes"

An Afternoon of March 20:
The Platte River near Kearney, Nebraska

"Nebraska" — from the Omaha or Oto Indian word for
"flat water" or "spreading water" describing the Platte
and Nebraska Rivers

Buttermilk sky. Deep blue space winged with white downy clouds shading to an ashy gray. The Sandhill Cranes come from all directions. There is nowhere to look but up in the sky, and nowhere to look that there are not Cranes, undulating wave upon wave of Cranes. Their calls precede them, announcing their skyborne waves flowing in immense V's of their orderly ranks, or, suddenly as if there were no North, East, South or West for them, they dissolve into a scattered alphabet, soaring on thermals which momentarily direct their course.

Cranes are among the oldest living birds on the planet. Fossil records place Cranes in Nebraska more than 9 million years ago, long before there was a Platte River, which by comparison, is a youthful 10,000 years of age.

There is nothing like it, no word to equate their sound. Nothing I have ever heard in all my life vibrates inside the ear like the calls of thousands of Cranes. But as I walk beside the Platte, I hear much lower down among the silvery cottonwoods the song of a solitary bird. A perch-

ing bird, a Phoebe takes up its solo, accompanied by the vast orchestration of Crane calls.

This little slender olive-gray bird of the Flycatcher family is possibly the first bird banded in North America. It was none other than John James Audubon who thought of putting silver wires on its legs so that he could record the Phoebe's migratory departure and return. And I am walking in one of the many places which are sanctuaries for birds, made safe for Phoebe and Crane by the Society founded in Audubon's name.

By the sound of its persistent call, Pheee-bee, humans gave the Phoebe its common name. But it is an uncommon one. The name "Phoebe" is that of a mythic titaness with dominion over the moon, a daughter of Uranus, sky-god ruler of the Greek universe, and of Gaia, first mother of the Greek earth. Phoebe's mythic pedigree, branches like the Crane's foot, an image which gives us the word from French *pied-de-grue* (foot of the Crane), and it includes her destiny to be the grandmother of Artemis, a goddess who began life in time before recorded time as the bird-goddess of the Stone Age.

The National Audubon Society purchased the property designated as the Lillian Annette Rowe Bird Sanctuary in the Platte River Valley (near Gibbon, Nebraska) in 1974 to assure the preservation of a portion of this vital staging area for Sandhill Cranes. Almost 2000 acres, the sanctuary consists of four major habitats — wet meadows/wetlands, tallgrass prairie, forest and riverine. By mid-March, between 250,000-300,000 cranes are on the Platte between Lexington and Grand Island. While here the Cranes gain critical energy for the rest of their migration north to their breeding grounds.

But far more ancient than the Phoebe's name are the Sandhill Cranes flying above the cottonwoods. These great primitive birds' ancient bones, found in Nebraska not too far from where we stand, are remnants of the Miocene Epoch when Cranes were alive and flying across this ancient river, itself a younger remnant of the Ice Age. The bones indicate they are the oldest living species of bird, virtually unchanged for nine million years. Indeed, as I look up at the masses of Sandhill Cranes they appear like giant flocks of Pterosaurs, the unfeathered (and unrelated) flyers of the early Jurassic Period, more ancient than the Crane's relative, the Archaeopteryx, said to be the first feathered flyer who holds the distinction of passing down to us an image of its feathers impressed in stone. Like our first writing on clay, the image is a lingering message — the bird's a message of dinosaur time.

It is almost dusk now, and twelve of us are inside the Audubon Society blind of the Lillian Annette Rowe Sanctuary. Our common bond is that we are birders, and we, like the Cranes, have "planed" here from all directions to gather at this spot. One of our group, a six-foot Russian from the Amur River region might claim the Sandhill as his own, for, part of this flock will go on to Siberian nesting grounds.

Origami Crane

Several of our group of Crane watchers are Japanese whose ancestors so revered the Crane as a bird of immortality that it is still an image of long life and good luck. There are hundreds of Japanese myths and legends of the native Cranes, and the image of the Japanese Crane *(Grus japonensis)*, now called the "Red-Crowned Crane," pervades Japanese art and literature, but the most famous modern story with roots in the ancient stories is the one of the little girl Sadako who, desperately ill from the effects of our nuclear bombs dropped on Japan, attempted to make a thousand paper origami Cranes as a symbol of life and endurance.

Before Sadako could finish her task, she died. Even today, the school children in Japan, in the U.S. and around the world still fold the complicated paper origami Cranes into a thousand Cranes to bedeck Sadako's statue, or to festoon their school rooms in her memory.

Among the other Americans are a professor, an ardent birder and scientist, plus several men and women who are environmental officials. We may, however, be someone like me drawn here by a once in a lifetime chance to see so many Sandhill Cranes gathered on the Platte River in this window of springtime, late March.

Twilight on the Platte

*Somewhere above me
the cranes with their
slow stiff wings were
pulling out of the river.
They were veering
towards the sand pits
to avoid the cottonwoods,
rising over the highways,
over the wetlands and
cornfields, ordering
themselves in loose Vs
above Kearney.*

Don Welch,
The Rarer Game

Inside the blind, we whisper as if the sound of our human voices could possibly overwhelm the insistent and constant calls of thousands of Cranes. Since earliest times, the Crane's cry has echoed and reverberated in human ears listening all over the planet. It is a call which has disappeared from those urban places we once called "civilized," and it has faded into the remote regions of the world. But, I think, its great range of notes must have lain at the back of my brain ever since primal ancestors stood upright in tall grass and searched with sharp eyes under heavy brows for Cranes. In this immense prairie twilight where only the western horizon is slashed with yellow light, rain clouds fill the darkening sky overhead, lowering, softly intertwined like the barbs of the gray feather I picked up in the field among the narrow hummocks of grass as we made our way to the blind.

A great flock falling like ashes has landed and settled in behind the blind, poised to make their short hop to the river before us. On the river, they will stay for their night's rest. Our guide looks out the back opening of the blind, then signals that we could photograph this enormous flock as they pick at the grubs inside the winter remnants of corn stalks before they will at last settle down on their roosting place, the shallow and wide River Platte.

Suddenly, as if a signal comes from some deep vibration of water below the earth inside the Ogallala aquifer, they rise as one bird from the cornfields, pouring their great numbers into darkened space. They flow across the sky, in rivulets like running waters of the night. Their skeins eddying and flowing in wonder across the sky, they mirror in their slow undulating chains the meandering waters of this eighty mile section of Platte River, lying a few miles to the south between Kearney and Grand Island, Nebraska.

This is all the river left of what once was a great distance of Crane roost. It is the last section of the river free of vegetation on sand bars and uncrowded by trees, the fractional survivor of the changes wrought by damming and field irrigating of what once was the entire river, free-flowing from Colorado and Wyoming headwaters, the two branches joining then going on to flow through Nebraska to meet the Missouri River

A rainbow arcs over the Platte River. The river is very shallow and sandbars dot the channels which offers Cranes protection from predators.

south of Omaha. Here is a perfect place for Cranes on their spring staging area where predators hidden by brush cannot steal up on them, and the water is appropriately shallow for the fastidious Cranes.

This river is called the "braided river" for a reason which writer John McPhee notes, when he flies over, observing it from 36,000 feet. McPhee writes of how the Platte seen from an airplane "resembles a braid of cable" as it channels among the gravel bars which are so numerous that the river is two miles wide. "Choked with rock, the Platte cannot transport its load in any but an awkward way, so it subdivides and loops and braids and hunts for passages through its own bed."

On the ground, McPhee and geologist Karen Kleinspehn search through the pebbles of the river to study the origins of the river's stone travelers. Kleinspehn picks up a rock she calls a "real diagnostic pebble." Like the Cranes in the sky, which have suggested to humans since ancient Greek and Roman times the alphabet and the formation of writing, this rock, a "graphic granite," is called so because "its interlocking crystals suggest writing" (McPhee quoting Kleinspehn).

We killed two geese and saw some cranes, the largest bird of that kind common to the Missouri and Mississippi, perfectly white except the large feathers on the first joint of the wing, which are black.

CAPT. MERIWETHER LEWIS
*Lewis and Clark Expedition
Journal entry April 11, 1805*

When Time Stops

For some reason, my quartz watch, always faithful to the hour, minute and second decides its time has run out. All three hands stop in perfect agreement at precisely six o'clock. But, I think, peering at its face within the dark shield of the blind, this timepiece halted at the very moment I watched the Cranes lift off from the field behind us. The mechanism (or at least its life blood the tiny battery) was no doubt overpowered by the timelessness of sky, water and bird. How could its hands go on chronicling mere human time when confronted by eons passing overhead in the form of these birds? Somatic time, or the life of the human body, has been compared by the Venerable Bede to a bird's soaring from darkness into a lighted hall then going into darkness again. Thus, his image of a lifetime is that of one illuminated moment: a bird's passage from dark to dark, of time out of time.

Calling incessantly, the Cranes are flying now in perfect symmetry, and I think: some day I might suddenly discover a word, one keen-edged word which would resonate sufficiently to describe the sound of 200,000 Cranes calling from all directions as they approach the Platte River near sunset, or as they rise at dawn as if they were one organism.

But as I search the sky considering words like "trumpet" or "bugle" or probing farther back in time to draw upon the medieval word "jangle," or to clamber farther down the centuries to Virgil's Latin "clamor" or Homer's Greek "clangor" and on to the Old Testament translation of the Prophet Isaiah and come up with "chatterer," I know I cannot find the exact word, *le mot juste*, the French who know a great deal about clarity in language might say. There is no word, no word I can find as I scroll through first my own then the vocabulary of poets and writers I know — ancient and modern — that could fill that quiver of sound I hear.

Scientist and writer Paul Johnsgard, a Professor at the University of Nebraska just some hundred miles or so down Highway 85 from here, has studied Crane vocalizations, the unison calls of mating Cranes, and the skyward calling of flocks of Cranes as well. He sums it all up very appropriately in his *Crane Music*, saying, the Crane's cry is "a haunting and somehow omniscient cry that carries both the authority of history and the urgency of reality."

An earlier naturalist, Aldo Leopold, famous for his concept of "land ethic," flexed his vocabulary in "Marshland Elegy" to write of a "pandemonium of trumpets, rattles, croaks and cries." But even great nature writers such as Johnsgard and Leopold, keen observers of Cranes that they are, really could never totally convey in words that almanac of sound. For it is a unique language which only coils within the spiraled trachea of Cranes, and no other.

The Crane family, *gruidae*, of which there are four genera and fifteen species the world over, and their order, *gruiformes*, composed of eleven additional families of birds besides the Crane, in other words their taxonomic classification given them on the model of classification established by Carolus Linnaeus, the Swedish father of taxonomy, began with the sound of their call.

The Latin word for them, *grus*, by which scientists still classify most of the Crane species, is a sound which was heard in the voices of one of the earliest civilizations. Linnaeus was tapping the roots of language, the Indo-European. *Grus* is derived from *ger-on*, the ancient Indo-European, and we hear the sound most plainly in the Greek word for Cranes, *geranos* and the Latin *grus*.

Furthermore, it is a sound you will hear in language elsewhere. "Put your ear close to a flower," writes garden writer Martha Barnett, "and you may hear the distant cry of the Crane" inside the word "geranium," some varieties red as the Crane's bare crown. And, whether or not Aldo Leopold was thinking of Crane lexicography when his wondrous creatures in "Marshland Elegy" put down in a Wisconsin cranberry bog, is a matter of conjecture. But his ear was close, not only to the calling Cranes, but to language which resonates with Cranes. For the cranberry is the Crane's own, called so by Dutch American colonial settlers for the bird's old world delight of the new world's berry. Thus the Dutch called it *kraanberre,* the word later adopted by English speaking settlers, preferring the Dutch derived word over their own "fen berry".

Words for Crane in Dutch *kraan (kraanvogel)*, German *kran (kranich)*, and, of course the English "crane" are so related that they signify a group of Germanic kissing cousins, within a great family of languages which scholars call Indo-European. There are at least several hundred language families the world over of which the Indo-European is only one, and the Germanic only a branch.

Add to the Germanic branch another European branch, the Italic which is composed of those languages derived from the Latin *(grus)* and

The unison call is a dramatic duet between the male and female of a mated crane pair. It is used as a territorial threat to neighboring pairs and is most frequently given at the onset of the breeding season when wetland real estate is being divided and defended. During this display, the calls of the male are completely different from, although synchronized with, the call of the female.

Dr. Bernhard Wessling
Crane Voiceprints

you will see the similarities in Italian *(gru)*, French *(grue)*, and Spanish *(grulla)*. Thus, you may identify a second group as distinctly related, with the Indo-European as the parent (or at least the grandparent) of modern Italic languages. There are six other branches of the Indo-European family's total of eight. In short, the languages belonging to the Indo-European family are spoken by people living from the sub-continent of India to the far west of the Aran Isles off the coast of Ireland.

Scholars surmise that beginning over 6,000 or 5,000 years ago, the Indo-Europeans whose parent language they dub Proto-Indo-European migrated from the steppes of Russia. Going west they invaded what would later be called "Europe" to the farthest point they could go west: to Ireland or to Iceland. Their linguistic descendents speak a language of one branch of the family and brought to the North American continent by the English pilgrims. Some of those descendents or those other immigrants assimilated into the English speaking culture going westward across Nebraska on The Oregon Trail. Spilling the English language into this North American continent also from east to west, they invaded the Native American land and erased many of their native languages as surely as did their linguistic ancestors the ancient Indo-European speakers. So many Native American tribes' languages have become "extinct," their last speakers dying and disappearing almost as rapidly as a biological species disappears. But scholars guess that at one time "1,800 to 2,000 different languages were spoken by Native Americans" when the pilgrims landed on the eastern shore (Waldman).

A Wide-winged Darkness

The wide-winged darkness descends on the Platte River now. Each of us is still, motionless inside this little space not more than fifteen by ten feet. The rough-hewn wood beams of the roof are low enough to make the six-foot Russian bend his head.

Our ears are tuned to the sound of Cranes. We are concentrating, trying to see, straining our eyes to make out the feathered shapes on the river before us in a darkness which envelopes all like a great and incomprehensible void.

It is a darkness we rarely sense nowadays in its completeness — and sometimes only when a power failure extinguishes the winking light of this electronic age. At dark times such as this, our primal forebears would light a fire stolen from the gods to illumine their cave of darkness.

As I strain to peer through one of the blind's small square openings, I think how long the Crane has been a storytale bird, one reverenced in myth, as a sacred bird particularly as a messenger of healing waters. Its meaning is embedded in the culture of immigrant speakers and in the original cultures of this continent, the Native American's. The Lakota Sioux, a tribe of these very plains healed by the Platte River, tell how the people of their mythic origins paused to hear the "voice of Cranes when they fly toward the region of the pines" (Walker).

I have seen the Crane's image in the dry American Southwest where many of these birds winter along another great river, New Mexico's Rio Grande in Bosque del Apache National Wildlife Refuge. They are living symbols evoking the divine waters, the rain and rivers which could turn the canyon floors green and trace its flow in dark patinas descending along the red cliff's face.

A Crane whistle,
Lakota Sioux, 1890.

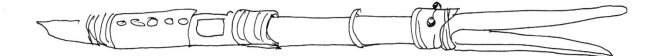

The Anasazi people who inhabited the Southwest of New Mexico and Arizona long before the Spanish arrived on horseback in the sixteenth century are the "people who went away," the "ancient ones" who disappeared leaving possibly because of nomadic invasions or drought which plagued the Southwest around the latter half of the thirteenth century.

But their houses of layered and crumbling masonry are still to be found in an immense area of the San Juan Basin, remnants elegantly coursed, puzzled over not only by the Spanish who saw them in ruins but by modern scholars who speak of the center of the culture in Chaco Canyon from which radiates invisible roads of the past as the "Chacoan Phenomenon." The Anasazi people made numerous objects from Crane bones, "awls, tubes and quite possibly beads" (Frisbie, *I.C.F. Bugle*). At the Chaco Visitor's Center, the people's many ceramic jars and fine jewels of turquoise are displayed. Outside on the living rock of the cliffs are mysterious drawings also telling of their presence and the presence among them of Cranes.

Although they may be seen in great numbers in Southeastern Arizona near Willcox during the January "Wings Over Willcox Festival," Sandhill Cranes do not migrate in great flocks to this part of New Mexico and Arizona —as they still do to the fertile Rio Grande center of New Mexico at Bosque del Apache. But they have left evidence of their presence in the dry wastes of northeastern Arizona near Canyon de Chelly, where their bones have been found. They did once come here though. One of the last historical reports of Cranes in this area was made as recently as 1926 by an observer sighting them near Canyon de Chelly. The unnamed observer reported seeing seven Cranes dancing "around on top of a clay hill, one of the birds in the middle" (Tyler quoting Phillips).

Crane petroglyph at
Twin Trail Ruin in
Canyon de Chelly, Arizona
—*Great Pueblo Period.*

The Sky-Water Spirits
and The Whispering Feather

Images created by the vanished people, their drawings on rock or their pottery designs, some elaborated with the dark shapes of Cranes dancing above the meandering form of a great snake, are no doubt an invocation to sky-water spirits to renew the dry world once made fertile by rain and to fill the canyons with healing surges of blessed water flowing like Nebraska's Platte River once flowed before it became to moderns of the industrial age useful mostly as "a river supplying power and electricity."

Among the Anasazi descendents are speakers who each speak words from distinct language groups. The Hopi, Zuni, Keresan, Tiwa, Tewa and Towa became the speakers of Pueblo Tribes of the Southwest whose civilizations arose after the Anasazi "went away" and whose resilient ancestors began to create once more the villages or pueblos mostly along the Rio Grande, clustered so like the civilization mysteriously extinguished. Among them, the Crane has survived in today's rituals and stories.

The act of storytelling for Native Americans is as formal and prescribed as a ritual dance. Many stories may be told at only certain times of the year, and stories fall roughly into two broad categories. There are those stories which "recover sacred time." And they reveal the creation of the world, of the tribe, unfolding certain secret knowledge, such as the way of healing, which only the tribe knows. The second type of story is the instructional one, told mostly for children, which reveals a deep knowledge of nature and nature's way. The storyteller, a Tiwa friend tells me, holds a "whispering feather" in the hand signifying that the tale is to begin (Dorothea Deal, personal communication).

One story told in the Tiwa language for the children of the Picuris Pueblo near the Rio Grande explains how the Cranes first migrated to the river. "Once," begins the story, "a flock of Sandhill Cranes lived up on the clouds in the sky, and they drank the water from

Crane designs painted on Mimbres pottery, New Mexico, *1050-1200 A.D.* (as redrawn by H.S. Cosgrove and cited by T.R. Frisbie).

the clouds and also built their nest upon clouds and they lived well"
(Tyler quoting Florence Merriam Bailey).

But one day, the story goes on, the Crane's leader persuaded the
flock to descend to earth. The birds landed far to the north of Picuris
probably in the place the Spanish called Sierra de las Grullas, the Mountains of the Cranes. They came down by a spring which was no doubt
one of the Rio Grande's sources. Before long, they drank up all the water
in the spring and they ate all the frogs and fishes. They moved southward to Taos, but once more they drank all the water and ate all the
frogs and fishes. A third time they moved, and it was to Picuris. But
this time they drank the water and ate the frogs and fishes, yet even they
could not drink all the water or eat all the frogs and fishes. Beside the
Rio Grande, a river "which could endure," they decided to stay (F. M.
Bailey).

Whenever we look at Native American myth, we must always remember they are valued stories, and they are secret ones. Stories presented to the world at large always have a slight change or twist from
the original which makes it not quite true to the tribe's own.

The Picuris story is obviously one from the "old days." Today,
though the Sandhill would most certainly not pass up a frog or a
fish, its greater diet consists of corn. The Sandhill's kindred North
American species the larger Whooping Crane, would be more
likely to "eat up all the frogs and fishes." The Whooping
Crane appears in New Mexico skies only singly or
in twos accompanying the Sandhills on migration, flying like a white blaze in the
sky among the ashy brown shapes of
the smaller gray Crane. Its image
drawn inside the caves and kivas, indicating its ancient presence, the
Whooping Crane is part of a restored
flock which is foster-reared by Sandhills from the Whooping Crane egg.
It was an experiment carried out by biologist Rod Drewien in the Grays
Lake, Idaho area near Yellowstone. He hoped to re-introduce a Whooping Crane population. It has been discontinued. However, that the
Whooping Crane had long traditions of migrating into this area may be
established by their prehistoric images in pictographs and on pottery,
pottery such as one of the Mimbres Period which show the Whooping
Crane devouring many fish, swallowing them whole as they pass down
its long neck.

Head of a Crane.

Although they still need the calcium of water creatures' shells — of snails and of mussels — today the Sandhills feast mostly on corn from the fields. And because of the great importance of corn to the Pueblo people, indeed corn is life itself, the Sandhill is associated with many of the Crane clans of the Pueblo in conjunction with their Corn Dance Rituals. In the 1850's, Cranes once covered the cornfields along the length of New Mexico's Rio Grande: "from Santa Fe to El Paso," according to nature writer Florence Merriam Bailey (quoted by Tyler). Thus, to the Pueblo Tribes whose chief subsistence has been the blessed corn, its

growth enhanced by the river, it is natural that their many rituals and stories center around the importance of corn and the seasons for its planting and harvesting when the Cranes appear in their skies. "Fortunately, Cranes do not eat ripening corn in the late summer and fall," say Jim Harris and Jeb Barzan of the International Crane Foundation. "Furthermore, they are wary of walking through the high corn stalks." Consequently, the Cranes are gleaners of cornfields, not harvesters, preferring the fields of leftover corn stalks, not the ripe corn of harvest time (*ICF Bugle*).

To the west of the Rio Grande, almost to Arizona, live the people of the Zuni Pueblo. In an origin myth, they tell of how their clans came into being. The "divine ones," the Shalako, appearing as great birdlike creatures, decreed that the Zuni tribe should be divided into clans. Among all the animals to choose from, one group chose the Crane because, while they were deliberating the choice of their particular animal, they looked up to see a "Crane flying by." From then on their allegiance was to the Sandhill Crane.

The Zuni Tribe, like many other North American Tribes such as the Ojibwa of the Great Lakes, has not only a Crane Clan, but it has a larger Band made up of clans. In the Zuni Tribe, Crane Clan members belong to the Newekwe Band or "Band of Wise Medicine Men." The one who was the first leader of the Band chose also membership in the Crane clan. From that time on the leader of the society has been chosen from the Cranes. Each member belonging to the Crane Clan reverently car-

Sandhill Cranes feed in the fields around Bosque del Apache, New Mexico. When allowed, Cranes have adapted well to agricultural habitats. They prefer short grasses or grazed pastures over tall prairies, since they rely on sight to protect themselves from predators. Corn and other grains readily add much needed body fat. Crustaceans and invertebrates are also important to a Crane's diet—snails and worms provide valuable proteins and shells provide calcium for egg laying. Cranes are opportunistic and will eat almost anything they come across, including insects, mice, voles, snakes, crayfish, clams, and frogs.

ries a wand having "two crane feathers attached to the upper end" as a sign of their membership in the clan and then, like the Bear People "became 'Holders of the Wand' — who bring the snow of winter and are potent to cure diseases" (Cushing). At certain times, only Crane Clan members may handle the Crane's feathers.

The relationship of the Crane Clan members to the species of bird itself is a close one, so close that "Cranes become synonymous with self," says anthropologist Theodore R. Frisbie, "because individuals are, by birth, equated with the magnificent birds. As children they learn the mythological ties by which they are bound to the cranes" (*ICF Bugle*, 1986).

Not only do the Cranes appear in their rituals, but they are also, of course, important in Zuni myth. One day all the corn harvest of the Zunis was taken from them by the Corn Maiden, a goddess, daughter of the Mother Earth, who was angry at the people for their ill-treatment of her. In most myth, around the world, anger of a god at humans is generally explained by the human's neglect of ritual or appropriate offerings to the gods. This is no doubt the instruction of the Zuni myth, for the Corn Maiden has hidden the tribe's store of corn and only a god such as Newekwe youth, or, if he is head of the clown society, Pai-yatemu, or the trickster solar god, Bitsisi, may search for the corn. Significantly, it is the Sandhill Crane who reveals to the god where the corn is hidden.

In another version of the story, the god is instructed by the Crane where to find the Corn Maiden who has hidden herself with the Zuni's store of corn. He entices her back to the Pueblo with the aid of his magic flute. The Corn Maiden's return is celebrated in the Molowia Ceremony held in early winter before solstice; the Corn Maiden is at that time of the year an invisible spirit, yet to return in her abundance to earth.

There can be no doubt that these first Americans, who have traditionally held animals sacred, are keen observers of each species' traits. The Crane's watchfulness, its ability to guard its own flock, in other words, to act as a guardian for the many, is a trait which appears not only in Native American myth such as the Lakota Sioux who made the Crane the marshal over the animals but in other cultures as well. The Greeks, such as Aristotle, separated by not only an ocean but thousands of years from the North American tribes, also extolled the Crane for its habit of posting guard, and set it as an example of the Guardian. Aristotle, writing of the signs of "high intelligence" in the Crane, took its wariness as one of the indications of its keenness. "When they settle down," he writes in *History of Animals*, "the main body go to sleep with their heads under their wing, standing first on one leg, and then the other, while their leader, with his head uncovered, keeps a sharp look out, and when he sees anything of importance signals it with a cry."

Living farther west from the Zunis on the mesas of Arizona, the Hopi Tribe's Crane Clan members perform a ritual which is to erect a "forty-inch tall stick topped by crane wing feathers and strips of corn husk" (Frisbie). The magic of a feather, it is said, is that it stands for the entire bird, just as the strips of corn husks may stand for the entire corn harvest. This Crane-winged staff is placed at the entrance to the Kiva, the below ground ceremonial chamber which represents the place of the ancient people's emergence into the Upper World. Their first emergence is from the womb of Mother Earth, a belief shared by many of the Southwest tribes.

Unlike the Corn Maiden, her daughter, this Mother Goddess is almost never depicted in "drawings or costumes." But in one rare representation seen by M.W. Stirling who was studying the myths of the Acoma Pueblo, the Mother Goddess is depicted as a "bird woman." With a bird's body and the head of a woman, she has a "red arrow shaped heart in the center of herself and of the center of the world" (Tyler quoting Stirling, *Pueblo*).

Crane dancing—
redrawn from a Hopi water
jar, Arizona, *19th century*.

When the Hopi's staff appears before the kiva, adorned with Crane feathers it is a signal that secret initiation is taking place for the Crane Clan. Members of the clan take the role of clowns, the trickster Koshares or as guardians who patrol the village during the ceremonials tied always to the seasons, some when the "white-eyed" tourists ladened with cameras descend en masse as spectators. But a far more important task for Crane Clan members which links them to the universe of myth and to the Greek god Hermes and his role as shepherd of the dead souls, is to conduct "the dead to the afterworld."

At the "Four Corners area," the interesection of four states, to the north and east from the Hopi Pueblo people, lives another major Southwest tribe, the Navajo. "Navajo" is not their word for themselves, they call themselves simply the Dine, "the people," and they speak of the "Deli Dine," the "Crane People," in their Athabaskan language, a language unrelated to the Pueblo's. The Navajo do not consider themselves, as do the Pueblo tribes, the descendents of the Anasazi, even though "Anasazi" is their own word, meaning "ancient people" with resonances of "enemy."

Navajo medicine bundle
utilizing a Cranebill.

Furthermore, the Navajo do not organize their clans into an animal clan system as do the Zunis or Hopis. Their clan names generally come from place names. However, the Navajo people have a very special ceremonial use for the Crane in the Cranebill wand used for their healing ceremonies (Bailey).

Even the hunting of a solitary Crane has a special sacred ritual to it. For the animal's bill possesses the spirit of the artifact made from the body. The Crane is to be taken only at its feeding place. And, no doubt because Cranes once came to the Navajo area but do not now migrate there, a Heron's bill may be substituted. When the Crane is taken, its bill is dried and cleaned of all flesh. Parts of the Crane's heart, lungs and stomach are also "dried and jewels inserted in them. " Then the parts are placed inside the dried bill "in exactly the same order as they are found in the body of the Crane." The reeds supporting the upper part of the wand should be obtained from Oraibi or Taos. The skin of the Crane's breast and back is to be slipped over the reed's joints. Pueblo foods are added and the entire wand stopped with "yellow ochre from a lightning struck tree." The pouch is wrapped with buckskin above the Crane's bill. This ritual completes the wand except for the decoration.

Each pouch above the Crane's bill is decorated differently to denote gender. There is a Cranebill for the female patient and a Cranebill for a male patient. The pouches must be decorated in the presence of the Flintway and Shootingway singers at the five night-chant ceremonies, the azee niilghe aineehgi, "making of the medicine preparation."

When someone in the tribe falls ill, the priest or medicine man attends the patient with both male and female Cranebills, placing the male Cranebill under or before a male patient and the female Cranebill before a female patient. Appropriate healing songs are sung "and the Cranebills used as medicine spoons" for the curative herbs. The patient in turn chants with the singer the "prayer to the gods" invoking them to release the sickness from the body, the illness itself which is brought about by the "magic influence of some divine power" (Franciscan Fathers).

The Franciscan monks who gathered the preceding information from the Navajos and published it in their *Ethnological Dictionary* in the Arizona of 1910, could never discover or know all the elements of Navajo ceremonies, for the secrets are held closely by the Navajo Tribe. But the Fathers would no doubt have not been surprised at the Crane as a symbol of guardianship and healing. In their own culture handed down to them from Europe, the Crane appeared in Christian religious beliefs since, and before, the time of their Order's founder in 1200, St. Francis of Assisi who was known for his particular reverence for birds and all animals. He is always portrayed with them.

St. Francis's holy image appears in the Santos (sculptures) and Retablos (paintings) on the walls and in the houses and Catholic churches of the Spanish Americans living in the Southwest who inherited their culture and beliefs from their ancestors, the Spanish explorers of the Southwest, explorers such as DeAnza, who riding northward in 1779 from Santa Fe entered a valley edged by the "Mountains of the Cranes," a range marked on 18th century Spanish maps of Colorado as the *Sierra de las Grullas*.

The modern maps describe the Colorado range as the "San Juan." Here people such as Donna Kingery monitor the migrating Crane flocks for the U.S. Fish and Wildlife Service. Cranes migrating south from the Yellowstone area stop off in the marshy fields near Kingery's home in Alamosa, Colorado as they have since prehistoric times. They go on to Bosque del Apache, New Mexico's Wildlife Refuge on that very Rio Grande River of their migrating traditions told of in the long-held stories of the Southwest Tribes.

Woodcut depicting a Franciscan monk in a monastery garden communing with animals—including a Crane. (*Encyclopedia Brittanica*)

"My little sisters the birds, ye owe much to God, your Creator,
and ye ought to sing his praise at all times and in all places,
because he has given you liberty to fly about into all places;
and though ye neither spin nor sew, He has given you
a twofold and a threefold clothing for yourselves
and for your offspring."

from
THE LITTLE FLOWERS OF ST. FRANCIS OF ASSISI
"Preaching to the Birds"

Messages of the Gods

The arts have received their increase and supplement from fowls. The Greeks have added four letters to their alphabet by marking the order of Cranes in their flight: epsilon, lambda, phi, sigma; whereupon (says St. Jerome) 'Cranes fly like the alphabet.'

REV. EDWARD TOPSELL
from *Aldrovandi*
1599-1603

Great concentrations of Cranes such as the immense number of Sandhills we may witness in springtime here on the Platte River, or in smaller concentration in the Southwest's Rio Grande in autumn, are an image of a long and nearly forgotten past throughout a great part of the world. Possibly because the Crane is such an ancient bird and such a large bird demanding a vast area for nesting, yet producing at most two to three chicks, "seven of the fifteen species found on five continents are endangered and others, though still plentiful are declining" *(Reflections)*.

In ancient Europe, the Cranes were once so plentiful they seemed to pull the seasons across the skies with their wings. Now, although he sees some positive comebacks, some Crane species have "been extirpated from several European countries in recent centuries" says George Archibald of the International Crane Foundation. Archibald speaks with the knowledge of one who flies all over the globe on behalf of Cranes, and he is arguably the most knowledgeable human alive when it comes to his beloved Cranes.

Not only moderns such as Archibald, but the ancient Greeks honored the Crane as well: the sight of them so moved the poet Aristophanes to look up to the birds, particularly the Crane, as the birds from whom "humans receive all their blessings." "The Cranes," says Aristophanes, "tell us of the season's passing, the time for sowing, the time for the shipmaster to put away his rudder and for Orestes to weave himself a warm cloak."

The Eurasian Crane is also called the "Common Crane". Swedish taxonomist Linnaeus knew this Crane and he used it as the holotype for all Crane species by classifying it as *Grus grus*. It was historically far more plentiful than it is today, but, like the abundant Sandhill, its counterpart in North America, the Eurasian species is also populous and is not endangered. No doubt, both species have survived because of their adaptability. Like the Sandhill, the Eurasian Cranes are flexible enough to change their habits, and "are able to forage in diverse habitats and to change their diet" *(Reflections)*.

Plentiful though it was in ancient times, the Crane was, even so, a bird of mystery to the Greeks and later the Romans. "Cranes," wrote the philosopher Aristotle, "come from the ends of the world." And just as its appearances and disappearances are mysterious to the tribes of North America, the Crane appears in the landscape of myth, sometimes in a very similar way, as it does in the classical world, for example, its connection to the power of healing. One particular image from myth which we see frequently in the modern world, the medical doctor's staff, is associated with the Crane, yet this link to the bird of wisdom has been lost to most of us.

In many ways the power of an image is apparently lost to us just as our perception of the origins of the Indo-European *ger-on* in the word we speak such as "crane." A word may be a transformed survivor of our culture's distant and ancient past, yet immediate as a word on this page. So too are the images and dreamtime stories, the myths of gods and goddesses, present beneath the surface of our everyday life. An example pointing to an enduring past may be found in the "caduceus" the medical doctor's emblem, an ancient symbol we might yet see today on a prescription form or the lapels of the army medical corpsman.

In the day-to-day rush, most of us rarely stop to think of the image's high antiquity or origins in ancient religions, or the caduceus's meaning rooted in myth. That "pause in the day's occupation" is sometimes left to artists and poets, or scholars — anthropologists and psychologists who mull over the myths of our own culture and those around the world, as well. We moderns may have very little awareness of the message. Yet unknowingly we are affected by its sign of therapeutic power, a spiritual message of healing which is as old as the beginnings of civilization itself.

The caduceus, a wand with two snakes twining about it and surmounted with a bird's wings — the Crane's — originates as the staff of Hermes, messenger god of the ancient Greeks who began his mythical life in Egypt. To the Egyptians of the Pharoahs' times, the god's talents belonged to the god Thoth, "lord of words," inventor of hieroglyphic writing. The Egyptians were quite aware that writing gives humans the power to endure into the afterlife, words of the dead becoming immortal, their deeds and their names preserved in images on stone. Significantly, the hieroglyphic image for the word "spirit" or "soul" is that of a bird which looks very much like a Demoiselle Crane often pictured accurately in Egyptian tomb paintings.

Sculpture of Hermes / Mercury holding the Caduceus, by Giovanni Bologna, Italy, *16th century*.

Egyptian tomb painting
with Crane in procession
—*Mortuary Temple of
Queen Hatshepsut
Dynasty XVIII.*

*Sometimes Nepthys
appears like her sister
Isis with the head of
a crane or Ibis. The
Queen of the West she
becomes the Queen of
the Night and of the
dead. Like Isis Hathor,
she is the queen of the
sky-world.*

EGYPTIAN MYTH

Thoth's sacred bird was a curved-bill Ibis, like the Crane a waterbird, but though it shares some natural traits such as flying with its neck out-stretched, it belongs to an entirely different Order of birds, the *Ciconiformes*, an order which includes many other waterbirds such as Flamingos, Herons, and Storks. When the Greeks living at that time, assimilated the characteristics of Egypt's Thoth into their own myths, he became their Hermes, at first a primitive fertility god whose sacred bird is the Greek's far more familiar waterbird, the Crane (Graves, *Myths*). The Greeks cherished the Crane, a bird they associated with the passing of seasons, and its arrival from Africa to Greece was a signal for the rites of the solar year to begin.

Hermes, son of Zeus and Maia, when only one-day old stole the sacred heifers of Apollo, also a mighty son of Zeus. Apollo sought his prize cattle, and he was directed by a "wide-winged bird" which Robert Graves suggests was a Crane. The great god found them in a cave where Hermes had hidden them. It is a story which has elements reminiscent of the Native Americans, the Zuni's story of the Corn Goddess' theft of their corn, her cache also revealed to a god by the Crane.

To appease Apollo's anger, Hermes gave the god a magic lyre which he himself fashioned. Apollo gained power over music with this musical instrument, and he was so pleased with the gift that he, in turn, gave Hermes a magic shepherd's wand. With this wand, Hermes became the messenger of the gods, a shepherd of souls with the power to heal, and thus to restore order to the world. This concept entered, as did most myth, medieval Christian belief, a mythic concept which endured because the works of artists and poets preserved the myth in their works, says mythologist Mircea Eliad.

The staff of Hermes, topped by a bird's wings below which two snakes twine about its shaft is an emblem of the god's principle godly task as herald to the souls of the underworld. To anyone who has watched a bird soar into the sky, the link with bird to the heavens is apparent, but to moderns reared in a Judeo-Christian culture and accustomed to the biblical image of the snake as sinister, the thought of a reptile as a healing creature may seem a paradox. However, ancient Egyptians and Greeks shared the custom of venerating the snake as a symbol of life's renewal. Its traits of casting-off an entire dead skin, and its nature to hibernate were to them an image of life beginning again. Thus, snake and bird having a natural and biological relationship share a cultural image of renewal.

Hermes' staff and his skills to regenerate were passed on to Asklepios, god of medicine, who learned his art of healing from the Centaur, Chiron. Hence, the modern doctor's emblem descended to us via Hermes from Asklepios (Aesculapius to the Romans), the first family physician, or as the Greek poet Homer called him in the Iliad "blameless physician". The Roman god Mercury took over Hermes messenger-god skills, and we are accustomed now to seeing Mercury in Roman statues as a winged man caught in the action of flying from here to there.

Egyptian hieroglyph for "b'a"— soul.

A bird-topped wand as a symbol of the human's desire to grasp a power to transcend the earthly bondage of the body and for the spirit to soar on high has its roots in a far older culture than the Roman or even the earlier Greeks. It is an image which is found in the cave paintings and carvings of the people who physicist Freeman Dyson says in *Nature's Imagination* "were more than ordinary hunters amusing themselves in front of a cave fire. They must have been trained artists of a higher culture." These people lived in Ice Age Europe some 14,000 to 30,000 years ago.

This particular image is what could almost be called a stick figure drawing, a male human who wears a bird's mask and who lies prone in front of a wounded bison. The animal, in contrast to the child-like and naive rendering of the human, is depicted in a painterly image, fully delineated and shaded as sophisticated in a way as an Impressionist's painting. The bison almost seems to be gazing with curiosity at the human who has laid aside, or dropped, a staff on which a bird perches. Many scholars, mythologists such as Joseph Campbell, and paleo-anthropologists such as Ian Tattersall alike have pondered over this drawing and other works of this great flowering Ice Age art so long ago.

Ian Tattersall of the American Museum of Natural History suggests that the image of bison and man is a "classic example of what must be a mythical scene. We may well see a myth recounted here," says Tattersall, "but a myth replete with many layers of meaning."

Some scholars take these cave paintings as absolute proof of the hunter culture. Others see the narrow passages, sometimes ending in great chambers such as in Chauvet Cave, or Lascaux in France or Altamira in Spain as the depiction of the womb of Mother Earth. New finds such as Chauvet Cave are constantly causing archaeologists to reinterpret their histories. But the relationship of human to animal is quite clear in the elaborate paintings of animals which sometimes coalesce into partial human form, hybrids of beast and bird.

Mythologist Joseph Campbell suggests that the prone stick figure man in an ichthyphallic state which is drawn on the Lascaux cave wall may very well be an early priest or shaman figure, and the bird staff a sign of the human's spiritual, possibly trancelike intimation of an immortal time and place. This very image may give a clue to explain the meaning of Ice Age cave art "which," says Tattersall, "was that of sympathetic magic, or the idea that symbolic actions may impact real life." Thus it is in this image of bird, bison and man that we most likely may see one of the oldest scaffoldings of ritual and myth: that of the hunters, the gatherers and the artists of the Paleolithic, the early Stone Age.

It was this primal age of the Paleolithic to which biologists Noble S. Proctor and Patrick J. Lynch point when they say that early humans were "first attracted to birds as a source of food." But over time, say Proctor and Lynch, this "fascination" led to the formation of myths. It is certainly one of the earlier "explicit references to birds". And among these caves in France and also Spain the image of a goddess with the gesture of the Crane was painted or carved from bone into figures in the round, predating the bird goddess of Neolithic times by "some 10,000 years" (Gimbutas, *Civilization*).

After the last Ice Age, the earth began to warm, shaping the habitat anew for the Paleolithic cave-painting artists and hunters in Europe. Very gradually over long periods of time they began to confront a new kind of forested habitat around the northern shore of the Mediterranean Sea. Animals such as the Bison, the Mammoth began to disappear. The enormous Irish Elk, whose existence we know of only from its bones and from Ice Age cave painters, vanished. With the disappearance of these huge mammals it is easy to surmise that birds which still appeared in enormous migratory flocks, became, as biologists point out "a major food source." For it was not only the bird's flesh, but the elegantly packaged protein-rich egg which nourished humans and their descendents of the old European civilization and, even today, most people around the world as well.

When the artist-hunter-gatherers of Stone Age Europe gradually began a major shift toward a new kind of civilization, moving away from the nomadic life of hunting and foraging, but moving toward the cultivation of grains such as wheat and barley, they began to form villages and to stay in one place long enough to make, among many significant advances, one profound advance, the creation of ceramics, clay figures, vases, and water jars. These creations according to archeologists such as Marija Gimbutas, hold vast meaning associated with myth and ritual. The culture arising in Europe during the post Ice Age warming period, Gimbutas designates as "Old European" to distinguish this autochthonous (or native) culture of early western civilization (6500 - 3500 B.C.) from their later blending with the invading, and alien, Indo-Europeans from the East — a mixture which ultimately formed into Bronze Age civilization of Europe with the ascension of the early Minoan civilization on Crete.

The Neolithic or new Stone Age people of "Old Europe" inherited from their paleolithic artist-hunter-gatherer ancestors the reverence for waterbirds. Waterbirds, the Cranes, Herons, Geese and Ducks are depicted in numerous artifacts. Because these people were "pre-literate" and their oral traditions and stories did not descend to us as have the mythic stories of Native Americans to their descendents, we have only the Old European artifacts to "read" in interpreting their culture. Recent archeological discoveries have revealed to us entirely new ways to look at pre-Greek Bronze Age civilizations in Europe.

Thousands of these artifacts discovered principally around and radiating northward from the Mediterranean Sea were examined by archeologists, Gimbutas among them, and interpreted as cult objects with recognizably hybrid human, bird and snake details. Notable among the earliest figures is the Bird Goddess figure of a woman leaning forward in the posture of a Crane. The largest portion of the figure's anatomy is a swelling posterior sometimes hollowed to contain what could only be a reference to the cosmic egg of the late Greek creation myth. The cosmic egg, laid by a "wide-winged bird" hovering in darkness and thus creating the earth is a guiding myth not only to the Greeks but is "universal from Africa to the Arctic" (Gimbutas).

A Mormon writer whose ancestors no doubt came over one of the very trails beside the Platte and who weaves its power into her story of birds of the Great Salt Lake and of her family, naturalist Terry Tempest Williams alludes to the cosmic egg in her work *Refuge* (1991). On one occasion Williams asks her Mormon grandmother "What [do] eggs symbolize?" The Grandmother answers: "For me, it is where life originates.

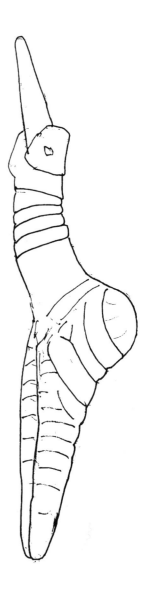

Neolithic Bird Goddess figurine showing forward leaning aspect of a Crane, *(circa 5000 B.C.)*.

In mythic times, the Cosmic Egg was believed to be held within the pelvis of the ancient Bird Goddess" (Williams).

The Bird Goddess image was transformed over several millennia until she became the later slim upright Greek ideal of beauty and proportion figured in statures of Hera, Zeus's wife, or Artemis, Zeus's daughter and the sister of Apollo. Thus she was no longer the overarching power, an aspect of the Earth Goddess but, like the moon over which she reigned, her light-giving power was out-shone by the sun-god, Zeus. In her beginnings she was definitely not the present day notion of beauty. These figurines were dubbed "steatopygous" by modern archaeologists revealing a twentieth century prejudice toward female ampleness. "Steatopygous" is an unwieldy hybrid term of Greek and Latin meaning "fat or over-ample behind," and it is still used as a technical designation for these little figures.

But Marija Gimbutas sees the term as "misleading and erroneous," for, she says, the hybridization of woman and bird endows the figure with "greater dignity" than the word "steatopygous" implies. These goddess figures demand the "dignity of the supernatural."

The bird element of the figure comes with an overly elongated human torso or neck sometimes topped with a bird's head. "A beaked and large-eyed goddess," she stoops forward in that leaning gesture of a long-necked waterbird — clearly a reference to the Crane. The large and swelling posterior could be an allusion to the Crane's "bustle" of long flight feathers drooping over the tail and giving the Crane that identifiable look.

Perhaps this look accounts for the relatively modern taxonomic feminine names assigned by scientists to species of Crane. The "Demoiselle Crane" has a distinctly female common name supposedly given to it by Queen Marie Antoinette who found this dainty and smallest of Cranes — despite which gender the Queen was looking at — as ladylike in its elegant plumed head and breast feathers. But the Demoiselle's taxonomic name has a confused gender implication of *Anthropoides virgo* which means "manlike maiden or virgin." Like the Eurasian Crane, the Demoiselle could have been seen by the migrating Indo-Europeans, and is still found in fantastic colonies in India.

The Sarus Crane of India, given its taxonomic name by Linnaeus is classified as *Grus antigone*, the descriptive name, "Antigone," a reference

Pre-Cretan European Bird Goddess. *(Brooklyn Museum)*

to a heroine of Greek tragedy, daughter of Oedipus the King. Because the Sarus Crane has a reddish bare neck skin, the allusion to Antigone evokes her mournful demise when "she hanged herself" (in some Greek versions she's buried alive). The largest Crane of all, however, has a name with a masculine connotation with *Bugeranus curunculatus* for the African "Wattled Crane." Its Latin scientific names combine the prefix "bull" (*bous* the Greek for bull) in the *Bu-* and crane in the *-geranus*. The curunculatus is descriptive of its large wattle or curuncle suspended from its lower mandible.

Perhaps because it represents a bird of power, mythologist, scholar and poet Robert Graves connects the African "Wattled Crane" to the Earth Goddess's power and her incarnation as a bird. Graves feels that most ancient love of the earth is embodied in reverence for the goddess. As a scholar he associates her loss with "man's irreligious improvidence" towards the "natural resources of the soil and sea." As a poet, and poets have a long and ancient tie to the Crane, he addresses the goddess, and he invokes her spiritual return:

> At dawn you shall appear
> A gaunt red-wattled crane,
> She whom they know too well for fear,
> Lunging your beak down like a spear
> To fetch them home again.

(White Goddess)

Whether they are shorter billed upland Cranes, or the longer billed wetland birds, Cranes are, of course, associated with water. As the Bird Goddess, or "the Mistress of Waters," she "is felt everywhere" among the Old Europeans culture, "on earth, in the skies and beyond the clouds where primordial waters lie. Her abode is beyond the upper waters, beyond meandrous labyrinths." And it is in the labyrinth of Bronze Age Crete we will later find this goddess and the dance of the Crane (Gimbutas).

A prime figure of the Bird Goddess, from the fifth millennium B.C. excavated from the Cucuteni site in Romania exhibits the motif of chevrons, incised V lines all over the clay form. Evoking the image of Cranes flying in a V, this motif is one of the major motifs used to signify the

Demoiselle Crane
Anthropoides virgo

Demoiselles are the second most numerous Crane with a population of about 230,000. Flocks containing 400 or more birds may migrate together from eastern Europe and the countries of the former USSR to India, Pakistan, and northeast Africa. While Cranes prefer to migrate at much lower altitudes, some Demoiselles must reach altitudes of 22,000 feet as they migrate through the high Himalayan mountain passes on their way to wintering areas in India, *19th century engraving.*

The fish does—HIP
The bird does—VISS
The marmot—GNAN

I throw myself
to the left,
I throw myself
to the right,
I act the fish,
which darts
in the water,
which darts,
which twists about,
which leaps—
All lives, all dances,
and all is loud.

The bird flies away,
It flies, flies, flies,
Goes, returns, passes,
Climbs, soars,
and drops,
I act the bird—
all lives, all dances,
and all is loud

part of a
Gabon Pygmy song

Bird Goddess. In the Crane's natural trait for the flock to fly in a V, there is another mythic connection with the later god Hermes or his Roman counterpart Mercury. At the beginning of the Christian era, the Roman scholar Hyginius writes that Mercury "invented the alphabet while watching a flight of Cranes" (Graves, *Goddess*).

A later Roman scholar and senator, Flavius Cassiodorus, elaborated on this concept in the fifth century A.D. In this translation, we may see the Crane's association with wisdom or knowledge, as well: "the god Mercury, discoverer of many arts, is remembered for his collecting [the letters of the alphabet] from the flight of Strymonian Cranes. For today Cranes living in flocks represent the shapes of letters by their inherent nature. Mercury reduced the shapes into a certain beautiful order. After he added vowels and consonants, the god discovered a logical way by which any mind seeking assiduously the inner chambers of knowledge might be able to find knowledge on high" (M. Yeakey, trans.).

Because the image of the Bird Goddess was created by its makers as a magical and religious object, both as a figure in the round and as painted or incised designs on ceramic ware, her symbol contained also three dots or lines, the first attempts, according to Gimbutas at "linear writing." Thus, the first whisperings of Old European goddess cults were formed, and language took on a ritual significance.

Thousands of years before the Old Europeans, the artists of the Paleolithic culture carved these goddess figures with an incised V signifying, it is said, the life-giving element of water. And the chevrons were connected into the form of a "meander," a word we use to describe a wandering river such as the Platte and also to convey the idea of a zig-zag design, as the "Greek key" design used by architects on buildings of Greek classical design or by the Native American snake-like designs incised on rock in the Southwest desert of North America, a symbol of water.

Her connection with a primary fertile earth joined with rain from the sky gives us what many call the Great Goddess, Mother of Nature. But as the cultures of the West (Old European) and the East (Indo-European) met and blended together the Old European's earth goddesses were overwhelmed by the successive invasions of the Indo-European's sky gods. Yet, she was not totally abandoned by the mother-goddess culture encountering the eastern father-god culture, only transformed. She became over time, as the great Minoan civilization formed on the Greek isle of Crete in the Bronze Age, multiple goddesses. Her many earth embracing attributes portioned off to goddesses who now had names and mythic family lineages, such as Phoebe, daughter of sky-god Uranus and earth-goddess Gaia.

Radically thinned down and sleekly proportioned, she became a goddess as powerful as was Artemis of the Greeks who was later transformed into the Roman goddess Diana, patroness of the hunt, a chaste rather than a fertile goddess as was her ancestor the Bird Goddess. Yet she still possessed the awful mythic power to slay the consummate hunter Orion whom the gods pitied and placed in the stars, where he still hunts, his constellation following the Great Bull *Taurus* in the night sky.

Multiple goddesses now, relegated to the domain of the nighttime moon rather than the original and long-held kingdom of earth, she is represented in triple lunar aspects: the New Moon by, for example, the maiden Kore; the Full Moon by the mature and fruitful Demeter, and the Old Moon, by the Crone as the terrible and fearful Hekate goddess of death and life, who receives dying bodies back into the earth womb. Because the moon was believed to be the controlling force of rain and water, the goddesses, embodied as the triple phases of the moon, became, rather than chief rulers of the wide earth, a wife or a sister of the new thunder-hurling father god brought into Europe by the invading Indo-Europeans.

The main thunder-hurling god of the father-centered Greeks is of course Zeus, the Roman's Jupiter or Jove. From on high Zeus looked down at the mortals and heroes pursuing their life on earth, some in battle such as the Trojans against the Greeks. The Trojans are described by Homer as "coming on with clangor and shouting/ As when the clangor of cranes goes high to the heavens." Ready to meet the onslaught of the Trojan onslaught are the Greeks who are massed together like "multitudinous nations of birds winged/ Of geese, and of cranes and of swans long-throated." *(Iliad)*.

Showing human failings, prejudices or preferences for one side or another, Zeus might very well hurl a bolt of lightning down to interfere with the actions of mortals, or sometimes, enamored with some human, he might appear on earth in any shape he chose. When on earth in his many shape-shifting guises, Zeus frequently pursued his favorite pastime of ravishing a maiden or queen when he felt desire for her. Taking a cue from the earlier Old European goddess culture of bird and bull, Zeus transformed himself into a bird, a swan, to rape Queen Leda, or into a bull to carry off Europa one of the earth goddess's descendents.

Earth Mother became Triple-phased Goddess of the Moon.

Zeus's many appearances in various forms, bull or swan, or shower of gold, and his many mythic rapes as Father-god have a historical basis in the actual attacks and conquests by the Father-god peoples of the Mother-goddess's numerous shrines, such as the Oracle of Delphi, which were scattered all over the Mediterranean (Graves).

One of the goddess's shrines and also one of the most important was found on the island of Crete, home of Europa and mythical birthplace of Zeus himself. Crete was the center of the earliest of what we may call civilizations — that is if we are using anthropologist Levi-Strauss's definition: a literate culture.

The Bronze Age Cretan or Minoan civilization of Crete is the civilization lost to us until the end of the Nineteenth Century when Sir Arthur Evans uncovered not only palaces and sumptuous wall paintings, but also stone tablets incised with a curious form of script. Mysterious as this writing was, one script which Evans called Linear B has been comparatively recently translated. The other script Linear A still holds many puzzles. In the Linear B script, we will see the "connection to the prehistoric" Bird goddess, "Mistress of Waters" and we will find her sacred bird's dance, the Crane's, hidden there (Gimbutas).

In the "meandrous labyrinths" of Minoan myth and in historical accounts as well, and in the designs incised or painted of the "Bird-goddess" are her symbol of life-enhancing water, the meander symbol winds inward like a labyrinth.

Mycenaean
terra-cotta figurine
13th/14th century B.C.
(Athens Museum).

At the Center of the Labyrinth

At the hidden center of the Cretan labyrinth, designed and built by Daedalus, first architect, dwells a half-man and half-bull, the Minotaur, offspring of Queen Pasiphae who it is said, mated with a great bull. The Acrobats, pictured in Cretan wall paintings, are the youth imprisoned by King Minos, Pasiphae's husband. They perform in art and history a ritual dance by leaping in front of the bull. This ritual dance is the *Geranos*: the Crane Dance.

According to myth and also to actual historical accounts by historian and biographer Plutarch, the young acrobats are the youth sent from King Aegeus, father of the hero Theseus, as tribute exacted by King Minos of Crete, who dominates the Mediterranean with his great power. Theseus swears to save the youthful prisoners and to slay the Minotaur. All of this he accomplishes with the help of King Mino's daughter, the Princess Ariadne who gives Theseus a ball of string which he unwinds as he searches the labyrinth. Thus, he is assured that he will find his way back. He searches the labyrinth. At last, he finds the Minotaur and slays it. And he discovers the youthful prisoners from his own father's kingdom whom he frees from their imprisonment.

His feats accomplished, the Minotaur slain, the acrobats alive and accompanying him, Theseus "then set sail," Plutarch writes, "with Ariadne and the youths." On his way home, "Theseus put in at the island of Delos" and there he rejoices with the youths by dancing a dance "called by the Delians, The Crane." The dance is performed around a horned altar said to be built by the god Apollo from the horns of animals sacrificed in dedication to his sister, Artemis (Graves).

The Crane Dance is described in detail by the poet Homer in *The Iliad* centuries later, after the Minoan civilization fell and the warrior culture of the Greek mainland dominated the Mediterranean. It is a dance which gives meaning to the dance as an ancient ritual, possibly one of the beginnings of dance for men and women dancing for the first time together. The youths are "linked, touching each other's wrists"

Labyrinth shown on a
Bronze Age Cretan coin.

like the echelons of Cranes who fly through their skies: "They circled there with ease" or "else again in lines as though in ranks they moved on one another. Magical dancing!" *(Iliad).*

Comparisons of the ancients intertwining in their "magical dancing," the *geranos*, to the actual meandrous labyrinthian structure leads us on to the link to the hidden Mistress of the Labyrinth, the prehistoric Bird Goddess, says Gimbutas, who singles out the Crane particularly as one of the Mistress of the Labyrinth's aspects. The Bird Goddess lived on, her presence apparent historically in "descriptions of early Greek authors" and her many artifacts "vase painting and finds in actual sanctuaries of Minoan and later Mycenean, then classical Greek civilization." Thus, "the Mistress of Waters," says Gimbutas, "survived in Minoan Crete, the Aegean Islands and in all areas where the Minoan influence was strong, including the Greek mainland."

Whooper dancing.

And the Crane Dance lived on, still performed today in dances of the Mediterranean people (Graves). Thus, the Europeans of the early Bronze Age and today could be said to be imitating the Crane's own dance of life, a dance particularly of spring delight which we have seen performed by the Sandhills here beside the Platte River, and which Cranes dance — as they no doubt did here thousands of years ago — and still dance, leaping some twenty feet in the air, not only in North America but in Europe and Africa, Asia and Australia — wherever some of the fifteen species of Cranes are found on five continents of the world. They dance and nest where they have survived the incursions of humans who at one time honored the birds of the air and animals of the Earth and who were living in a world in which they were vastly outnumbered by the creatures they revered.

When a Time Out of Time Ends

The labyrinth, its likely origin a prehistoric conflict between Crete and Attica, is a fitting mythic image of the uncharted material world in which humanity was born and which it forever struggles to understand. Consilience among the branches of learning is the Ariadne thread needed to traverse it. Theseus is humanity, the Minotaur our own dangerous irrationality.
EDWARD O. WILSON
Consilience

By eight P.M. darkness envelops the Platte River, and its thousands of Cranes, secure upon their roost mid-river still cry out, their calls reverberating in the labyrinth of our ears.

The Audubon leader whispers, "It's time to go." And we leave the blind in single file, each of us forever changed. We walk across uneven ground in the dense and utter blackness, not two by two or three by three, and certainly not in the wide sociable ranks of the people we were when we arrived here at the Lillian Annette Rowe Sanctuary before night-fall.

In the darkness, we are silent and alone, walking one behind the other more like a band of primal humans following an invisible path.

in the sand
saved, the dance
of the sandhill crane

JIM KACIAN

All our species' legacies walk with us. On these plains the invisible presences of Omaha, Pawnee, Sioux seem to walk beside us in soft moc-casins. For three hours we have known what life is like on this continent before our European ancestors arrive, and the birds far outnumber our species.

By the time we reach the waiting van, we will become more like the booted pioneers who stopped here to quench their thirst for the Platte before they set out again along this, the Oregon Trail to fulfill a destiny they fevered for in the rich lands beside the Pacific or to die in the cold snowy Rockies beyond the Great Divide.

But we will not forget this field and the river as they have become on this one day of equinox, an overwhelming wilderness of land and water scarcely populated by us, but filled with the night sounds of thou-sands upon thousands of Cranes.

Whooping Crane
Grus americana

Wood Buffalo National Park. Northwest Territories, Canada

Calgary Zoo Alberta, Canada

Last Mountain Lake Saskatchewan, Canada.

Gray's Lake NWR Wyoming

Necedah NWR, Wisconsin

Monte Vista NWR Colorado

Cheyenne Bottoms, KA

Platte River Nebraska

Quivera NWR Kansas

Bosque del Apache NWR, New Mexico

Salt Plains NWR Oklahoma.

San Antonio Zoo

Aransas NWR, Texas

Howtzfa NWR, Florida

Kissimmee Prairie, Florida (year-round)

CURRENT SUMMERING & WINTERING AREAS.

CAPTIVE POPULATION

MIGRATION STOPOVERS

MIGRATION ROUTES

FORMER MIGRATION ROUTES.

ULTRALIGHT FLIGHT PATH

CURRENT MIGRATORY

Adapted from: *Cranes: Their Biology And Conservation*, edited By David H. Ellis, George Gee and Claire M. Mirande. Department of Interior, National Biological Service, 1996.

Coastal Bend

When I see a Whooping Crane in the marsh
at Aransas, fully erect, glaring at an intruder and
trumpeting an alarm call that can be heard
up to two miles away, there is no doubt in my mind
that the marsh belongs to the Whoopers.
It is our responsibility to keep that marsh unchanged
so that the Whoopers will continue to survive.

TOM STEHN
U.S Fish & Wildlife Service Whooping Crane Coordinator,
Aransas National Wildlife Refuge

An Early Morning, January 18:
The King Ranch, Texas

Boarding a tour van, the "Running W" brand of the King Ranch flowing like a rattlesnake across the van door, I make up the final person on the tour as I climb in beside the driver. It is 8:00 A.M., and I have arrived just in time to make the tour. I drove here in a borrowed Ford Explorer, a "Don't Mess With Texas" sticker on its bumper, a University of Texas Longhorn decal on its rear window.

The drive south from Corpus Christi is only forty miles or so as the Crane flies, but all the way here, over roads straight as a draftsman's pen line across the vast flatlands, I was anxious. I did not want to miss this opportunity to go on a winter birding tour on this incredible ranch. The King Ranch is a place of dreams — always big dreams, but sometimes, dreams gray as a South Texas sky in winter. And filled with a harsh history as well: with the terror of bandit raids, the stress of drought, and the eternal ambush of Mesquite which threatens more than once to take over the land from the cattle — as the cattle take over the land.

The young man behind the wheel of the van is far more than our driver for the day: he is the King Ranch's own wildlife consultant and he's Ron, a biologist, who knows his birds and frequently speaks their language.

Because I learned of this occasion to join the tour just as I planed into Corpus, I had to forego my first priority: an annual visit to Aransas

The King Ranch brand.

National Wildlife Refuge to see the wintering Whooping Cranes. That's scheduled for tomorrow, however. Today I'll be more than happy to catch sight of many perching birds, raptors, and waterbirds, and to see where the Whooping Cranes once wintered. There will be abundant mammals: antlered White-tailed Deer and wild boar-like creatures, Peccaries, called "Javelinas." The Zoo at home has two of these fellows, the male they call "Gregory Peccary" and the female "Olivia de Javelina."

Sandhills roaming along a South Texas woods.

"The land seems to emit an immutable life
—apart—transcending ownership—
beholden to no higher order
than the Order that brings
the rain and the frost, the heat and the cold.
Its self-sufficiency, its independence overreaches
humankind's relatively brief million years
here on earth, making us mere custodians
during our minimal time."

JOHN CYPHER
retired Assistant President
of the King Ranch

There are plenty of waterbirds to see, but there's very little possibility that we will catch sight of Whooping Cranes, Greater Sandhills, possibly, but Whooping Cranes no longer winter here. They did once. As late as the 1920s a flock of sixteen Whooping Cranes wintered here on the King Ranch. This group of Cranes was one of "three groups known to be in existence," says Faith McNulty. The other two flocks of the vanishing Whoopers could be found at what is now the Aransas Wildlife Refuge on the Blackjack Peninsula north of Corpus Christi, and also to the east in the Louisiana marshes. All told the three groups made up an estimated count of forty-nine Whooping Cranes which were thought to be alive in 1918.

Other dividends await us today, however, for the King Ranch is a working ranch, and we will no doubt encounter some of the cowboys, the "kineños," the King's men, who will be herding the mahogany red Santa Gertrudis cattle — a breed of cattle developed here in the "rincon de Santa Gertrudis" — the first breed of cattle developed in North America. The development of the Santa Gertrudis was a long and complicated one: originally cross-bred from the tough hot-weather cattle of India, the Brahman, and the cool-weather British Shorthorn cattle, the Ranch produced a new species. After these numerous cross-breedings and line breedings, the Santa Gertrudis became one of the many firsts for which the ranch is known the world over.

Medieval farmyard bestiary with Crane showing a bucolic camaraderie.

We see that tame and domestic Cranes do every year lay a stone in their nest among their eggs. Making no particular choice of stone without difference. It is doubtful they would do so in the wild.

ALBERTUS MAGNUS
in *de Animalibus*
(*1206-1280*)

Wild Horse Land

They afford one of the most beautiful instances of animal motion we can anywhere meet with. They fly at great height, and wheeling in circles , appear to rest without effort on the surface of an aerial current, by whose eddies they are borne about in endless circles of evolutions.

MAJOR STEPHEN J. LONG
upon seeing Sandhills, 1823

Located along the coastal bend of South Texas, its southern boundary stretching toward the Mexican border, the King Ranch is famous most of all for the immensity of its land holdings. Big enough to put Rhode Island into and still have room to spare, the four ranching divisions of the King Ranch comprise a fantastic 825,000 acres. The desert ranch is so big that it is practically a self-contained biome of live oaks, their gnarled trunks and branches clumped together in tight dark green fists called "mottes," and of Mesquite, trees beside brackish ponds surrounded by Saccahuiste, a salt grass, once a particular favorite place for Whooping Cranes.

When this vast area was acquired in 1853 by the Rio Grande steamboat captain, Richard King, it lay in what is called the "Nueces Strip" to describe the waterless, deserted stretch between the Nueces River at Corpus Christi in the north to the Rio Grande Texas border to the south. To the eastern border is what is now part of the Intra-coastal Waterway protected by that great barrier island Padre Island. Besides "Nueces Strip" there were other names. Some called the area "Wild Horse Desert" to denote a bare place of Texas Longhorn cattle and feral horses. Others, who no doubt had tried to cross the strip, called it the "Desert of the Dead." Most of the early Spanish families, originally granted land in the New World by the Spanish king, gave up their attempt to ranch it and let their horses and cattle wander away. The scraggly herds of Mustangs and Longhorns which steamboat Captain King found here in 1853 were the feral descendants of the wandering domestic Spanish herds.

The problem, of course, which made this land so hostile to humans and to their domestic animals, was lack of water. Captain King, however, was resourceful enough to find and to do the impossible: he discovered fresh water, and he urged it from the earth. The story goes that King, on his way to Corpus Christi, rode northward through Wild Horse Desert. Halting after one hundred twenty-four miles of tough riding, he happened by chance to stop at the first fresh water to be found: the Santa Gertrudis Creek, an oasis of Mesquite shade and fresh water in the desert. However it was not until 1899 — thirty-six years later — that

I part out the
thrusting branches
and come in beneath
the blessed and
the blessing trees.
Though I am silent
there is singing
around me.
Though I am dark
there is vision
around me.
Though I am heavy
there is flight
around me.

WENDELL BERRY
"Woods"

King's son-in-law Robert Kleberg finally succeeded in bringing in an artesian well.

After King found the fresh water, the Santa Gertrudis Creek, the Captain decided to turn this desert strip into a ranch. He continued his shipping and freighting business with partner Mifflin Kenedy, whose surname is still on the map as Kenedy County, Texas, the enormous county which together with Kleberg County — King's son-in-law's name and the name of his descendants and the present owners — encompasses all of the Nueces Strip.

King began buying up great chunks of land from the departed Spanish landowners, and set about damming creeks, conserving water and purchasing cattle to stock the land. In one Mexican village where he went to acquire cattle, he found the inhabitants and their animals starving. With a single great decisive move, he not only bought all the cattle to bring back, but he brought the entire population of the village back to his ranch, the men to serve as cowboys. These villagers are the forebears of the present day kineños who still work the ranch and who married and had children.

By the end of the Civil War in 1865, King married the daughter of a minister, Henrietta Chamberlain, who herself after forty years surviving him would become a major force in the ranch's survival. The ranch in the "Desert of the Dead" of post-Civil War days under King had grown to 146,000 acres and was populated with thousands of cattle and the Mexican villagers, now with U.S.-born children, who worked the

Jane, Jane,
Tall as a crane
The morning light
creaks down again

Edith Sitwell
Facade 1923

cattle. But only one of the King's five children stayed on the ranch — daughter Alice — who married Robert Kleberg.

Although today innumerable human "snowbirds" descend upon South Texas in their mighty campers to winter over, little is known of the wildlife of this area in King's day, particularly the birds. Now the snowbirds of Minneapolis or Milwaukee set forth with binoculars and field guides bent on adding to their birder's "life list." They may spot an Inca Dove sitting on a branch, and duly record its presence, some of them celebrating a "Life First."

But in the days following the end of the Civil War when the great ornithologist Henry Dresser visited South Texas, he contributed new information from his ramblings and notetakings which would enhance the world's rare knowledge of the Whooping Crane. Dresser's "Notes on Southern Texas" appeared in *The Natural History of the Cranes* by Edward Blyth, revised by W.B. Tegetmeier in 1881.

Dresser sighted some Whooping Cranes near San Antonio. Furthermore, he notes that he was "told the Whooping Crane was occasionally seen on Galveston Island and the mouth of the Brazos River." He also saw nine or ten birds in Mexico on the Rio Grande delta. Far-flung over the area of Texas and into Mexico though it was, even by Dresser's visit in the mid-1860s, the Whooping Crane was not a common sight. The confusion between this rare great white-feathered Crane, the Whooper, and the smaller gray-feathered Sandhill reigned. Indeed the lumping together of these two Cranes with other waterbirds such as the Herons was rampant, as it still is, sometimes unhappily so.

The King Ranch Whooping Cranes

Ron stops the van, and I with the other passengers, each of us encumbered by binoculars and camera, climb out. We're about to have some spectacular wildlife experiences. The first bird we sight is almost hidden in a clump of marsh grass surrounding a dense swamp just to the right of the road. Hidden in the grass is a Yellow- Crowned Night Heron, on the alert to grab a tasty Texas toad. I can make out its great eye turning in its head as it peers into the brackish mud and viscous water of the pond.

The yellowish crown and plumes are difficult to see, as the Heron conceals itself in the dense marsh grass. But I see its orange legs, its three toes, and the extended back toe of a tree-nesting bird which distinguishes it from most species of Cranes that ground nest. It holds onto a log, in perfect Heron balance, ready to strike.

"Yellow-Crowned Night Heron," a voice says beside me. "*Nycticorax violacea* of the family *Ardeidae*. I've been spotting this fellow right here over the years."

I turn to look at my companion. He is a tall Texas gentleman with a professorial and knowing look.

"You come here often?" I ask.

"Lived in nearby Kingsville all my life. The city of Kingsville was born on the Fourth of July 1904 — that's when old Henrietta King, Richard's widow of forty years gave enough land to make a town, and enough town to have the railroad: she wanted to ship her cattle north to market."

He takes another look at the Heron through his binoculars. "My parents moved here then and I came along not too long after that, grew up, went to university, and returned to teach in the college here. My students call me Professor Kingsville".

"Well, Professor Kingsville, have you ever seen any Whooping Cranes here on the King Ranch, or at least outside the Aransas Refuge?" I ask.

He lowers his binocks and seems to be considering the question as he looks up at the sky, his eyes forever on the search for birds. "Once or twice — maybe three times at the most in forty years. When I stopped hunting and became a birder," he answers. "I've seen one or two flying over the marsh on Padre Island. Not often, just a couple of times.

"But when I was a boy, my father told me there was a whole flock on the King Ranch. It seems old Captain King's grandson Dick — Richard Mifflin Kleberg — fell into the habit of riding over to the lake on the Ranch where thousands of waterfowl collected in the winter. He'd spot a couple of Whooping Cranes here and there among the multitudes of birds. He grew intensely interested in them. In fact, he was interested in many, many things.

"Like his father before him, he was a lawyer. Not only was he a lawyer, but for a time, he was a Texas Ranger. In World War I, he skulked the Tex-Mex border as an intelligence officer, tracking any of the Kaiser's agents — Germans — who might be operating in Mexico.

"Well, his work as a spy stood him in good stead: he was stealthy enough not to disturb the Whoopers — the wariest bird imaginable. They came every winter, some stayed through the summer, and he believed that some actually nested there. First, he counted three Whoopers. More came each winter. By 1919, he got close enough at three hundred yards to spy sixteen Whooping Cranes on the Ranch. Now, when you consider that all the Whooping Cranes anywhere was at a low count of forty-nine — that included the Aransas Flock and the few birds still alive in Louisiana — sixteen Whooping Cranes in one place was an important find. Important enough for old A.C. Bent to write up Dick's sighting them in his book *North American Marshbirds.*"

"What happened to them?"

"The flock dwindled, falling off each year, fewer and fewer of the big white birds. But, as I understand it, that was happening all over. Up at Aransas too — you know, the Aransas Wildlife Refuge. The Refuge wasn't established to protect the Whoopers until 1937. And even though they were protected — at least in the wintertime — the headcount kept falling. By 1942, the entire number of Whooping Cranes in the world dropped to the all-time low of sixteen birds — some say fifteen. The entire population the same number as Kleberg once saw on the Ranch."

"You're right about that," I say, thinking of that well known statistic. "But what happened to the King Ranch flock specifically?"

"You'll have to look at Robert Porter Allen's study for the National Audubon Society. He completed it just after I returned to this area from college in the fifties. In fact, if you're going to look at Whooping Cranes at Aransas tomorrow, you need to understand what Robert Porter Allen did for them."

I wrote Allen's name down in my notes and underlined it. I'd come across it before in Whooping Crane research. Every text I looked at seemed to cite Allen.

Professor Kingsville looks down at me, seeing my notes. "You know they used to serve Crane for dinner on the trains down here when I was a young fellow. My father, who was quite a self-taught scholar, often quoted Havelock: "The best meat that King or Kaiser would eat — Cranes, lampreys, and good sturgeon."

"Have you tasted Crane?"

"Never. Some people liked them, but I thought, too stringy, not enough meat. But, say, speaking of Cranes, take a look at those guys up there." He points to the gray winter sky. "Greaters, *Grus canadensis tabida,* I suppose."

Like letters of the alphabet, three Sandhills ride the thermals, their dark primary feathers arcing like slender fingers for the loft they need to make their peaceful circling over the immensity of the Ranch.

"I could watch them all day," he says, eyeing Ron who is signalling us to return to the van. Just as I turn my gaze from the Sandhills and the Heron and the marsh, I notice wide swashes coiling through the pale green algae on the surface. The marks look as if an enormous two-wheeled vehicle made wide tracks through the shallow marsh pond.

"Those tracks," I say, "how did they get there? What could have made them?"

"Why those," my companion 'Professor Kingsville' says, "those are Alligator trails — *Alligator mississippiensis.* It ranges from the mouth of the Rio Grande all the way to North Carolina. Look right down there."

I look down at the ditch beside the road. Just four feet away from my toes at the edge of the road, I see two knobs arching over two very

Cranes prefer soaring in thermals (updrafts of warm air) and will circle until they reach a desired altitude, somewhere between 3,000 and 5,000 feet. Once reached, the cranes leave the thermal and begin to glide, slowly losing altitude. They then find another thermal and repeat the process.

As deer in nets are by the hunters taken, so snares and slings are shaped to take the Cranes.

VIRGIL

large eyes gazing up at me, seductively as any ancient reptilian memory. The alligator observes me from below, steeped in its great genetic memory, but, like me, who is fading backwards, it is hatching its current plans.

When we are back in the van, Ron starts the engine, and scanning a dense clump of huichache bushes, eases forward, chugging just a hundred feet along the road until he stops and switches off the motor. A great hush falls over the group, each of us leaning forward trying to guess what Ron has seen.

"Look in those bushes to your left," he says, "down low."

All heads swivel left. There they are, a family of four Javelinas, peaceful as can be feeding near a beehive.

I lower the window slowly and look out at boar and bee. I am filled with the smells, the sights, and the sounds of earth time. A great scroll of time seems to be unraveling before me, marked with alligator tracks in algae, sawgrass, mud, and sky, the airborne Cranes, the grazing mammals. It is as if the hieroglyphic of all species is suddenly written large for me to read. From the unifying zone of algae, grass, and tree to the complicated spiral of higher vertebrates, up to the soaring Cranes; all seem to fly together and explode into life with a spark of methane gas floating from the marsh.

A Map of Life

With this great ranchland edging against the sea, you may imagine the dawning when the margin of land and water gave way, creating growth in the brackish marshlands and waterponds. It is possible in this singular vastness to read the phylogeny, the swarm of life, the many species, and their interdependence, in the signs plotted on earth-time's chart. First, the sea grasses' determined march up the dunes on the eastern shore. Plants and hard-bodied animals appearing with the red algae of the Cambrian Period.

And then, the land surfaces colonized by insects, the beehive a swarming delegation of the insects — so numerous that they yet compose half of all the species alive today, many insect species still unknown. You may read the beginning of forest and swamp in the Mesquite tree near the marsh, and then, the alligator tracks appear with their lumbering amphibian effort.

In the alligator's gaze is the living stare of the vertebrates; the amphibians leave the first footprints; on a path leading to the Archosaurs, the ancient animal founders of the great Dinosaur dynasty of the Triassic Period. Their domain came to an end in an early extinction mostly of marine animals and some plants, the Permian extinction. It was die-off preceding that other great mass extinction in the later Cretaceous, the time of the Dinosaurs, when mighty though they were, the Dinosaurs succumbed, their end brought about, it is surmised, by the impact of a celestial body's earth-fall.

Far to the south, the Gulf waters rolling into the shoreline of the King Ranch will also roll across the great Chicxulub Crater, filling that slingshot shape of the Yucatan, a hook of coast which yet shows partial traces of the great asteroid's impact, a crater estimated as one hundred eighty kilometers in diameter.

Within the spiny bristles of the Javelina — their fossilized bones known to date back twenty-two million years — is the acrostic of the first small mammals co-existing with the Dinosaurs such as the mighty *Tyrannosaurus rex* and those mammals whose tiny ancestors survived the great reptilian extinction of the Cretaceous. They grew and lived on, their early descendents witnessing the birds that are now, like Alligator

Yea, the stork in the heaven knows her appointed times; and the turtle [dove] and the crane and the swallow observe the time of their coming, but the people know not the judgment of the Lord.

JEREMIAH
Old Testament

63

and Crane, living survivors of the Dinosaur extinction.

Far along the chart, coming almost like an eyeblink in the long gaze of life are those stages of life's adaptation. Some are thought to be gradual changes, some are thought to be great leaps and sudden metamorphoses. Life, or at least human life, has definitely changed from the past to this present moment, a past when our fellow hominids are thought by those anthropologists who hold to the African "Eve" theory of migrating from Africa into Europe.

The Javelina, also known as the Collared Peccary or the Musk Hog, is the only wild, native, pig-like animal (members of the *Tayassuidae* family, true pigs are members of the *Suidae* family) found in the United States. Ranging throughout the Chihuahuan and Sonoran Deserts of southwestern Texas, they can also be found in southern New Mexico, southwestern Arizona, and Mexico. Up to 60 inches in length and 20 to 24 inches in height, the adult male weighs between 40 and 60 pounds. Their fur is very coarse and colored a grizzled black and gray with a dark dorsal stripe. Javelinas usually travel in a band from six to twelve. They are most active during early morning and evening when it is cooler.

With a powerful musk gland on the top of the rump, their odor is always apparent—you may smell a javelina before you see it!

Certainly there is a time when the hominids are finally anatomically modern humans: the Cro-Magnon. They are the artists/cave painters and their offspring of Old Europe who learn to cultivate grasses, wheat, and barley and whose territory is eventually invaded to merge with the Indo-Europeans who come into neolithic Europe with the use of the wheel and with a knowledge of breeding domestic cattle and horses. Each animal, it must be remembered, is "alien" or reintroduced to the New World.

And you may find those domesticated cattle in their descendents the first domestic species of North America, the Santa Gertrudis. Named for a patron saint of the Spanish explorers, who like the Indo-Europeans eons ago, brought their domestic cattle and horses with them, the Spanish, of course, to the New World leaving them to wander in the desert.

At last, the town, is formed. The Latin for town, *civitas*, is the word from which we get "civilization." A town made of citizens and cut from the fabric of land that was the King holdings, Kingsville, settled and growing with early Texas pioneers of European stock, as are "Professor Kingsville's" parents. And the town surrounded by ranchland in the "Desert of the Dead," a desert which is now truly alive.

Ron starts up the van, and we ease along the road leaving the Javelinas to their wildness, totally at ease and unaware of our existence. Rounding a curve with a slowdown to a crawl, we pass by a magnificent Santa

Gertrudis bull who stares at the van as if to confront a
possible rival. Farther along, a gate stretches across the road.
We're about to enter another section, a division of the ranch.

Cranes may fly almost
50 m.p.h. during level,
flapping flight, but prefer
to soar, especially during
migration. Cranes ride
thermals so efficiently,
they have been seen
flying over Mt. Everest
(28,000 feet).

I wait for Ron to stop so that he or one of us can get out and open
the gate. Instead of halting, he proceeds at a steady speed just fast enough
to tap the gate lightly with the van's bumper. The entire gate swings
precisely, arcing on a maypole-like contrivance. As we pass on one side,
the gate whirls around and closes behind us.

"A bump gate," Ron laughs at our astonishment. "They're all over
the ranch. The cattle have never figured out how it works, but some of
the horses have."

"It's not easy for us humans to figure out either," my friend Professor Kingsville says. "When I was younger, I'd drive through too fast,
and just like a boomerang, the gate swung around and broke my tail-
lights more than once."

Ron edges to the side of the road and stops. "See that hive there," he
says pointing to the right. "Killer bees — *Apis mellifera sceutellata*. They
were introduced to this hemisphere by accident from Pandora's Box you
might say — for someone back in the 1950s opened a box of Africanized
bees in Brazil — and they've been moving north ever since."

I roll up the window and peer at the hive through the glass. My skin
crawls. In a swarm, the bees may be deadly, their story just another
horror story of an introduced species.

"Our only hope," Ron says, "is that those deadly guys will hybridize
with our gentler bees the black and brown honeybee — *Apis millifera* —
and lose their killer instincts. Incidentally our honeybee is like the killer
bees in that it is also an introduced species, brought here by European
settlers."

A hundred yards in front of us, two kineños cross the road on horseback. Their two mounts ease through the sawgrass and vanish into a
motte of Live Oak, two mounted shadows of the past.

It is inconceivable to me that an ethical relation to land can exist without love, respect and admiration for land and a high regard for its value. By value, I of course mean something far broader than mere economic value; I mean value in the philosophical sense.

ALDO LEOPOLD
Sand County Almanac, 1949

We near a corral, a "corrida," a roundup is in progress. Inside the corral abutting a wide field, a dog of indeterminate breed chases at the heels of cattle running about in a dusty arena while kiñenos direct the dogs with hand-signals and whistles. Overhead, the three Sandhills re-appear, whirl above the corral, then begin a gradual slanting descent towards the field. Cupping their flight feathers to finger the wind, they hover lightly, then touch ground with the long-legged, light-bodied agility of Cranes — landing like sudden god-like messengers of the gray Texas sky.

They land in a field nearby where a man labors at cutting away the omnipresent Mesquite, a task begun in Captain King's day. Ignoring the human presence, the birds fold their wings to pass among a herd of Santa Gertrudis, their red-crowned heads and grey-brown feathered necks appearing above the heavy shoulders of the dark red cattle, a startling contrast of light-bodied grace to the fleshy magnificence of the Santa Gertrudis, each with the lithe rattlesnake-like brand, the code of the "Running W" on its flank.

Nature and Art Converge

In ordinary speech, "to converge" means simply the act of meeting at a certain point — our word "convergence" is a getting together. But life scientists use the term "convergence" to mean something quite significant when they are engaged in thinking of similarities of certain unlike organisms.

In short, creatures may evolve that are totally unrelated, their adaptation occurring over quite dissimilar paths through, sometimes, eons of time. But these creatures may acquire remarkably similar features.

Biologist Ernst Mayr's example of convergence is the "independent acquisition of the same features by unrelated evolutionary lineages, the acquisition of wings by both birds and bats."

Mayr's point I sometime mull over at dusk when I watch our neighborhood bats, those flying mammals, skitter through the darkening air, swooping up their insect feast. While higher up are the Night Hawks fluttering through the twilight sky on white-barred wings — each one — bird and bat flying along and engaged in a similar task — catching insects which are also flying.

In literature, writers use a device that is the convergence of similar qualities by unlike entities to create an image, that is a "metaphor."

In other words, when the poet looks at the moon and calls it a "ghostly galleon," as Alfred Noyes does in his poem "The Highwayman," he is creating a concrete image by using the convergence of two unlike things which share similar qualities. The moon like the ship seems to be sailing through the clouds, and the "ghostly" descriptive word reminds us of its paleness. Two abstract unlike entities converge into one image — a metaphor.

Thus, when I see the spectacle of Crane and Bull, a commonplace one to any South Texas rancher, I am moved by the convergence of a most ancient past and a stirring present; it is an image of art and myth — the light-figured bird's grace beside the plodding bullock's power. "Earth Shaker" the early Greeks called the bull in a metaphorical phrase, attributing its might to the powerful earthquakes which rocked the Island of Crete.

A sketch of Celtic altar piece: *Esus Cutting the Willow Tree.* The Willow and the Cranes are associated with the water's edge, and the pillar may possibly depict the destruction and rebirth of the Tree of Life in Winter and Spring. The birds may represent spirits of the process of change.

Before me is a scene very like the tableaux vivants in which people, and sometimes animals, take their place on a stage. Unmoving, they gather to replicate with living bodies a work of art, generally an old Master's work such as Leonardo da Vinci's "Last Supper" so favored in the annual pageants of Laguna Beach, California. Here on this ranch as in Laguna Beach, life appears to imitate art.

Whenever humans find themselves in places so overwhelming as the King Ranch, the only way to grasp the immensity is to turn to myth or art. And, in one instance the Romans of Caesar's Celtic Gaul (now France) did so in order to try taming the ineffable forces which went bump in the dark strange Druid-haunted wood of the conquered land.

What I'm seeing alive here before me evokes a most ancient mythic memory, one painted in caves or chiseled in stone. One so ancient that it goes back much farther than Caesar's first century A.D., to the early Stone Age times of Old Europe when Cranes are depicted in earliest art together with the bull's image. Both bird and mammal are associated in the triad of the Great Goddess, whose earliest representations are hybrid human and bird, the Bird Goddess, mother of earth and sky.

The particular work of art which this scene before me brings to mind is a curious work of chiseled stone, a Celtic altarpiece dated around the year 1 A.D. It is a work which puzzled the Roman conquerors of the Caesar's time, and it is still puzzling to many scholars. On one side of the piece is chiseled the figure of a man whom some scholars, unable to come up with something better, call a "woodcutter," a man in the act of cutting branches from a sacred willow tree. Busy at his work, the man appears so like the kiñeno in the field hacking away, not at willows but at the intransigent Mesquite, a vegetation which has a freehold on the ranchland as solid as the King Family descendents, the Klebergs, who are now part of the corporation, the present-day owner of the ranch.

On the other side of the altarpiece, an artwork though in Roman style, and considered to be "pagan" by the Romans, is depicted a mighty bull. On the bull's back and head, three Cranes, light as the Sandhills before me, stare out across the heavy weight of the bull. Surmounting the scene of bull and birds, the unknown Celtic sculptor has carved in the Roman alphabet the words *"Tarvos Trigeranus"* — "Bull with Three Cranes." On the opposite side is the single word "Esus" carved there to identify a Celtic hero-god, part of a triad of gods. The Roman poet Lucan who lived in bloody Nero's time himself, speaks of the gods as "horrible" and the third god of the triad, Taranis, "as no less cruel than Scythian Diana" — the Roman goddess of the hunt and of the moon, her counterpart the Greek goddess Artemis. Roman and Greek goddesses traced their pedigree back to the Crane goddess, the "Bird Goddess" of the Cretan labyrinth, Artemis, the dancing goddess of the geranos, and the human dance in imitation of Cranes.

These ancient secret codes and riddles, the signs and symbols of myth and the image of a secret god preserved in art are impressive as the brand encoded on the flanks of the Santa Gertrudis bullock.

Visual images such as the sculptural icon of Esus do not reveal secrets to the unknowledgeable viewer — that is the person who is not "in the loop" of power and knowledge. But the written word may give away secrets — anyone who has tapped into the Internet's World Wide Web knows that — but even though writing as well as visual images may be used to preserve secrets, words though apparently telling a simple story may hold beneath the surface just as much an indecipherable magic as the riddle of the visual.

One famous riddle poem in the *Book of Ballymote* apparently about birds and seasons holds a riddle to convey the great knowledge of the Celts. That the Celts had secrets unknown to the Romans is revealed in recently discovered Celtic medical instruments showing that they were far ahead of the supposedly technologically superior Roman conquerors. For it has been recently found by archaeologists that the Celts had a very advanced medical knowledge with the existence of instruments indicating that they knew how to perform such delicate operations as cataract surgery.

Not only a knowledge of healing but another closely held secret in every culture, that has discovered it, is the alphabet: the power of the word — or at least the word's components. In the secret code of the Ballymote, the Crane is linked to the "month of wisdom," the wisdom of the god Mannan Mac Lir, son of the sealord Lir. And the secret alphabet of the Celts was wrapped in the magically empowered skin of the Crane.

Take but the letter which the Crane does make from the verse, then sense from it her flight does take.

MARTIAL
(Marcus Valerius 40-108 A.D.)

Sculpture of a Crane standing on the back of a turtle as a guardian to the entrance of an African village, *Bambara tribe.*

The alphabet I use to spell out the words of my Ranch field notes is no longer a secret one. It is a script, however, which in the beginning held a kind of magic power, a power to write and a power to "cast a spell."

In his work *The Spell of the Sensuous*, David Abram reminds us of the origins of the word "spell." Once, known writing held such a potent force for the writer that the word could mean both "to enchant with a spell," or to shape individual letters into words — "to spell a word."

As I hurriedly write my field notes, I look up to see Cranes lift off from the field, leaving us and the hefty four-footed cattle earth-bound, and I think of how this alphabet on the page before me was believed by the Romans to be invented by their god Mercury, the god with whom they associated the Celts' hero-god, Esus. Inspiring Mercury to make this momentous invention was simply the elegant flight of Cranes.

A *New York Times* article on the front of Sunday's "Business Section" questions if the "King Ranch, a Way of Life, is Riding into the Sunset" *(Times)*. Feature writer Barbara Whitaker answers that: "The tradition has been under assault at King Ranch for years," and she reports that the last Kleberg, Stephen, son of Richard, has left the management. Now a corporate entity, the King Ranch may have a different administration but as Robert Kleberg's biographer John Cypher says, "the land transcends ownership."

One evening John Cypher walked out into the Ranch, and spell-bound as I with this immense place, he writes: "The land seems to emit an immutable life — apart — transcending ownership — beholden to no higher order than the Order that brings the rain and the frost, the heat and the cold. Its self-sufficiency, its independence overreaches humankind's relatively brief million years here on earth, making us mere custodians during our minimal time."

Tonight in the vast Texas sky, the planet Mercury will wander in its fiery path so near our sun. A "ghostly galleon," the moon, in one of its three phases will hang over the Mesquite and tug at the Gulf as it rolls to shore at the eastern edge of the King Ranch. The moon's pale light will illuminate the slumbering Alligator, alert the Night Heron, and shine along the spiky bristles of the Javelina. The white dazzle of thousands of Snow Geese will stir, while the dark red cattle and the gray Sandhill Cranes will slumber beneath the message of the land, the sea, and the planets circling among the distant stars.

White Crane
Spreads Its Wings

Investigating the winter life of the Whooping Crane
meant a great deal more than simply watching the
activities of the birds themselves. Those activities were
only the signpost that pointed to the interrelated patterns
of the entire environment. Maps were studied, the influence
of winds and tides checked, marine animals were collected,
and their identity, relative numbers, size, apparent age
and sex considered under one set of conditions and then
under another. With planned patience we sometimes
waited weeks for anticipated conditions to appear.

ROBERT PORTER ALLEN
On the Trail of Vanishing Birds, 1957

The Morning of January 19:
Corpus Christi, Texas

Corpus Christi — Latin for "body of Christ"
Texas — from Caddo Indian word "Tejas" for "friend" or "ally"

On an ordinary city street running parallel to the leisurely splendor of Ocean Drive is a green and white street sign with the single message to hurrying downtown Corpus traffic: "Carancahua St." This street sign is the only evidence you will see other than in a museum in all this vast land of Gulf and palm tree that an Indian tribe by the name of Carancahua (or Karankahua) once held this territory. A powerfully built race of people, the men over six feet tall, strong and fleet enough to run down a deer or brave and fierce enough to appear suddenly in a Spanish explorer's armed camp, bodies covered with alligator grease, there is not a single Carancahua Indian left.

They didn't give in easily. Early explorers described them as a proud people who, of the first Americans inhabiting the Coastal Bend country of South Texas, held to their own traditions. "The Cronks," as they were called derisively by the white settlers — busily taking their land away from them "fair and square" — could survive on harsh land where no white man could survive.

Possibly because they held to their old ways, never yielding to French or Spanish explorers, Mexican landholders or Texas settlers, they were systematically exterminated. If they did not die by the diseases the Europeans brought them, they were brought low by musket and cannon fire.

A modern visitor to Corpus Christi will see not even a recognizable genetic descendent walking the streets. The Carancahua are an extinct people and the great "white bird," another native American living on the Coastal Bend, the Whooping Crane, like the Carancahua, held to the old ways, and also followed the Indian people to the edge of extinction. But unlike the Carancahua who had the added detriment of humankind's diseases factored into their equation (which like the Crane's also included the gun), the Whooping Crane somehow survived — thus far. But even with encouraging "comeback" statistics, the great Crane is, unlike its kindred species the Sandhill, still considered to teeter on the edge of extinction. It is truly an endangered bird.

I hear the government is buying up the Blackjack [Peninsula] for a pile of money just to protect a couple of them squawking cranes. They tell me they ain't bad eating, but there is no open season on them.

A TEXAS LANDOWNER
IN 1937
(quoted by Robert Porter Allen)

75

I drive past Carancahua Street because I'm on my way to the public library where I will hold in my hands the plain looking standard library-bound book *The Whooping Crane* by Robert Porter Allen. Published fifty years ago, Allen's *The Whooping Crane: Research Report No. 3*, like its subject *Grus americana,* is still a classic. It is a massive research effort in both field and library to compile observations of nature and to include historic eyewitness accounts of the Whooping Crane, no doubt one of the most massive research reports on a species ever conceived and carried out by one individual.

A modern explorer on the hunt for the Whooping Crane, Allen flew in a small plane over twenty thousand miles, mostly in arctic areas where he skimmed above tundra and ice packs. In Texas and Mexico, he drove six thousand miles in a bone-jarring Jeep all over the dusty roads leading to wherever the White Crane had been sighted. As Audubon Society's first Research Director and with twenty-seven months in the field, "one month rubbing elbows with Mexican vaqueros, the next drinking tea with a family of Eskimos," and twelve months in the library, Allen finally sat down to write up his report. His educated conclusion on the Whooping Crane's distribution over a hundred years before his time in the 1950s is that its migration pattern could be described fairly accurately as "beginning their northbound migration from points separated by the width of the North American continent." From "the Gulf of Mexico, Texas and Louisiana," and from western Mexico, "100 miles from the Pacific Ocean, while still other migrant groups set out across the Appalachians from wintering grounds on the Atlantic Seaboard." (*T.W.C.R.R.*)

Allen used historical reports from the Atlantic shores to the interior of the continent, which he found acceptable, to make his conclusion. One report by an early visitor to the Corpus Christi area over one hundred seventy years ago is the kind of evidence Allen might not accept, however, because the writer did not specify if the Cranes were white or gray. This report is by Berlandier.

Jean Louis Berlandier, a Swiss-trained botanist aboard a vessel sailing off the Coastal Bend in March of the year 1829 was becalmed near Port Aransas for over a week. This interlude, a pause from the work of his scheduled mission to survey the Mexican boundary, allowed him the leisure to look around, to go ashore and explore the area. Thus, his journal gives the modern-day reader clear and valuable descriptive information about the way it was here on the Coastal Bend, for we know from his exacting journals that he visited Corpus and Matagorda Island of South Texas over one hundred years ago. Berlandier writes a clear picture of the land, when he follows along the Texas coast:

"In the springtime, particularly in the rainy season one travels entire leagues over ground covered with from one to two feet of water. The region abounds in water hens, various species of ducks, cranes, egrets and several other birds of the wading and web-footed family....

In the cavities carved in the sand among the dunes one finds fresh water, where we renewed our half-exhausted supply. We then crossed over the northern point of the bar where the Carancahuas are often found camped to catch turtles when the bays are not sufficiently furnished with fish."

Interestingly enough, here present in Berlandier's notes are wetlands, Cranes, Carancahuas — all have mostly disappeared. That Berlandier actually sighted Cranes, Whooping or Sandhill we may be fairly sure. This is true not only because he was a scientifically trained naturalist, but because of his being native to the European continent. Had he been an English naturalist of the same period, we would not be so assured. For two hundred years before Berlandier visited these shores, the Crane, though it was historically present in England, was no longer endemic to the British Isles. Today it is listed in field guides such as *Collins' British Birds* as a very rare visitor.

The probable cause of the disappearance of the Cranes in England? The draining of the wetlands particularly in the East of England around Anglia. East Anglia was, in some ways, the same profusion of wetlands Berlandier saw here — some of which are still around. But a major portion has been filled in by cities, highways, and farms, and the area has become increasingly arid. In addition, the problem of whether or not an historical report is a true and accurate sighting was a major problem faced by Robert Porter Allen in his extensive research on the whereabouts of the Whooping Crane. He went back to the 1600s with reports such as David Pieterzoon Devries' of white Cranes at the mouth of the Hudson River, and he moved onward to his day in 1952. Allen searched through every eyewitness report in early settlement days, but the earliest report anywhere in the North American continent in which he could have absolute faith was not made until 1722 when, admittedly, an English-born observer saw a Whooping Crane. But the observer, Mark

Whooping Crane
drawn by
ALEXANDER WILSON,
(with Lousiana Heron, Pied
Oyster-catcher, and Long
billed Curlew), *19th century.*

Catesby, rather than describing it in words, which he also did, depicted the Whooping Crane in a careful delineation of its head and neck. This was the only kind of evidence Allen accepted.

Yet evidence of Allen's life may be found not only on a library shelf, but in the field and waterworld of South Texas as well. There, the distant pink sparkle against green marsh grass will reveal much more. For the Roseate Spoonbill *(Ajaia ajaja)* which you see feeding at the edge of Corpus Christi Bay, with the spatulate bills, highly specialized and elongated, belong to a living image of Robert Porter Allen's lifework. These birds Allen called "Flamebirds" are survivors at peace while five o'clock traffic "homeward burns" just five hundred yards or so from their flamboyant feathered shapes. If they take wing, they seem to set the gray Gulf sky ablaze with their pink and magenta coloration.

You won't of course see the Cranes beside the city's bay as the first explorers and later Berlandier probably did — you'll have to go north some fifty miles to see the Whoopers at Aransas Wildlife Refuge. Where, also like the Roseate Spoonbills, they will be feeding at the margins of wetlands, but in solitary, splendid, and protected isolation.

As Research Director of the National Audubon Society, Robert Allen Porter became the "leading authority on species threatened with extinction." By 1957, when his book *The Trail of Vanishing Birds* was published by McGraw Hill, Allen had dedicated over twenty-five years of his life to the study and preservation of the Roseate Spoonbill, the Flamingo and the Whooping Crane.

He was such a dogged field researcher that the intense pain of crippling disease could not slow his far-flung hunt for the Whooping Crane in the North American continent. Before that search began in 1945, he was already credited, arguably, with single-handedly as an Audubon executive saving the Roseate Spoonbill from extinction.

Calling himself a "Seton Indian" as a youth, Allen's boyhood hero, Canadian writer Ernest Thompson Seton so fired his imagination that he spent in some ways — because of his immense talents and persistence — what could seem more than one individual's allotted lifetime in preserving the miracle of waterbirds in the American landscape. He spent enormous amounts of time — and energy — in the field and the endless hours writing about them, or depicting them in drawings.

But even with his amazing share of artistic talent in literary and visual portrayals, Allen knew, as he said in his own words, "A naturalist must hogtie his imagination and search for facts" *(Vanishing).*

A Search for Facts: The Ecozone

The facts I needed about the King Ranch flock, I found almost at once in Allen's *Research Report*, on page eighty-one. Allen estimates the flock's number from 1912 up to 1949:

YEAR:	1912	1917	1922	1927	1933	1949
KING RANCH:	20	16	9	6	3	0

Allen relied on Richard Kleberg's report, but he also found other reports from ornithologists who visited the Ranch. Clearly, Allen always liked two sources at least for one fact. The facts showed a steady decline, and Allen never looked at a fact without analyzing what it meant.

Some reports from experts hazarded a guess that "over-grazing" by cattle may (or may not) have lowered the water table in all of South Texas as the area became increasingly arid. But Allen concludes there were never "great numbers of Whoopers" in this region. In fact, he concluded that since early historic times it was never an extremely populous bird anywhere on the North American continent. Those that were here migrated south in winter. His educated and thoughtful guess was that "the gradual losses did not occur in Texas, it would appear, but elsewhere, along the flight lines."

Although Allen used all the technology available to him mid-twentieth century — primarily photographs and aerial surveys, he could not have had the long-range image of planet earth as a self-contained sphere surrounded by a thin layer of air. From Allen's perspective, mid-twentieth century in the words of poet/philosopher John Koethe, the "world was yet uncircled."

The science of Ecology was only then beginning to make inroads into biologist's thinking. Ecology, from "the Greek *oikos* ('household')," as Fritjof Capra tells us, is the "study of the relationship that interlinks all members of the Earth's Household."

Whooper family.

Relative size: comparison between Whooping Crane and Sandhill Crane.

This system was only beginning to emerge as an influential method of regarding the planet, even though the concept had been around since 1866, when "German biologist Ernst Haeckel defined it as 'the science of relations between the organism and the surrounding outer world'" (Capra).

Now, we use spin-offs, newly coined words such as "ecosystems," "ecozones," or even "eco-tourism" to express these concepts. In truth, Allen was fully aware of this relationship of organism to environment in a practical way when he studied the Whooping Crane's behavior and searched for its whereabouts.

But it took a single photo, "Earthrise" beamed back to us twenty years from Allen's time and which Allen didn't live to see: the 1970s photo by our first "Extraterrestrials" — the Apollo Astronauts circling earth and moon. Then, and only then could earthbound humanity truly comprehend the Earth from a global perspective: that we and all life are organisms, a network of life dependent upon a finite world of air, the biosphere, inhabiting our "household" on planet Earth.

In the early 1980s, about thirty years after the Whooping Crane's nesting area was found in Canada, biologists on the ground and in the air, working as a team tracked a Crane family from Aransas. To accomplish this, they used radio telemetry. However, their instruments could only help them keep track of the three Cranes from a fairly short distance. They would lose them in rain or snowstorms and spend agonizing hours waiting for the storms to subside. Then they would lose them again. Only through sheer luck did they sometimes relocate them. This pursuit team's efforts were well-documented in a 1982 National Geographic Special aired on television.

But now, we have satellite tracking. "The migrations of Cranes," says Jim Harris of ICF, "have delighted and mystified people for millennia. Today satellite-tracking studies have changed neither the delight nor that sense of mystery .... Tiny transmitters placed on the backs of Cranes, satellite receivers high above the earth and the rapid communications of E-mail and the Internet have combined to reveal each stage in the migration." But even with the advantage of the satellite-tracking technology, Harris seems to underscore what Allen clearly knew when Allen writes of the Cranes and the "interrelated patterns of the environment." Harris continues that "satellite studies have emphasized what we already realized; fragility of the ancient Cranes in the modern World." (*Bugle*, November 1998).

Allen's conclusion about the ever narrowing "thin line" of Whooper migration northward from Aransas was not made by idle earth-bound guessing. Allen went into action. He began a "media blitz" along the flight lines from Texas northward to Canada with the hope that he could halt the gunning down of Whoopers on migrations.

Earlier, Allen could be credited with almost singlehandedly — as an Audubon executive with the Society behind him — studying and preserving the Roseate Spoonbill. But the Whooping Crane's perilous state took a joint venture with Audubon and the U.S. Fish and Wildlife Service, together with an army of biologists, birders, and farmers — plus all the technology available in the postwar 1940s and early 1950s. The monumental effort to save it made the Whooping Crane the most famous bird in North America.

He began by spreading the "gospel" of the Whooping Crane up and down its last flyway from Texas to Canada with a Canadian Fred Bard helping to the North. Allen's dedicated belief was that if he got the facts out to the public — particularly the white Crane's value and its nearness to extinction — coupled with a clear description of the appearance of the bird — farmers and hunters living up and down the migratory flyway would help protect the Crane and stop their random shooting of it. Thus, he felt that he could at least make some inroads on the terrible statistics, the "kill records" he compiled from many sources. He had researched accounts from the Atlantic coast to the Platte River in Nebraska up into Canada. Perhaps, if he couldn't altogether halt the haphazard gunning down of the Whoopers, he could at least diminish the slaughter.

The facts seemed constantly to grow more appalling. When Allen returned to this Texas Coastal Bend area in 1946 after serving aboard a minesweeper in World War II to take on the investigation of the Whooping Crane's whereabouts in the joint Audubon/U.S.F.W.S. venture, the data on the Whooping Crane population was certainly dismal. And knowledge of the bird's history throughout the North American continent was hidden and scattered in numerous accounts of eyewitness reports. These reports, beginning in the 1500s, were frequently unreliable. Furthermore, and almost as important as the facts of the Crane's

In Texas, the Whooping Cranes are seldom seen above the three-foot contour line, just beyond sea level, whereas the Sandhill Cranes are rarely observed below that line.

ROBERT PORTER ALLEN

location in history, were the meager facts of its behavior, a knowledge of the bird so thin as to be non-existent.

"In 1945," he writes twelve years later in *Vanishing Birds*, "when the Whooping Crane Project began, the immensity of the problem and our ignorance of the facts were appalling to contemplate."

The headcount was steadily declining, a crash-course rate that alarmed every scientist and birder who knew about it or who cared about the survival of this most majestic North American avian species. Humans had already seen the consequences of a species on a headlong dive into extinction, most notably in the devastating disappearance of a single species which had in the 1800s, only a century before their time, been one of the most numerous species of birds anywhere in the world. The Passenger Pigeon tumbled out of the skies, bodies filled with buckshot or caught in nets, its numbers diving from uncountable millions of individual birds to a single flock in its exponential fall into extinction. In September of the year 1914, the last Passenger Pigeon, Martha, died in the Cincinnati Zoo and closed a page on American plenty.

By 1945, it was fairly clear to anyone such as Allen who could put a knowledgeable eye to the perusal of facts that the Whooping Crane was about to soar off the edge of the living world.

Allen counted sixteen migratory Whooping Cranes on Aransas and nine on nearby Matagorda Island, the center of the Carancahua tribe. By

Cranes can maintain normal body temperature while standing for long hours in near-freezing water. Blood vessels in their feet constrict so less blood needs to be warmed. Arteries and vessels in their legs are right next to each other so the colder blood is warmed before it reaches the body.

Allen's time the island was used for bombing practice by the U.S. Navy. Furthermore, the Louisiana population, non-migratory resident marsh birds, stood now at only two birds, "all that was left of a flock observed by John Lynch in 1939." Allen added up a "total count of perhaps twenty-nine Whooping Cranes in all." *(Vanishing)*.

Allen's conclusion that Whooping Crane count was dropping or had fallen to zero in some places as had the King Ranch flock for example, was not due to the increasing aridity of the region, which admittedly was a factor, but primarily because they were shot down along the flight lines. He defined these lines as a migratory corridor now reduced from two or possibly three flyways of the past colonial

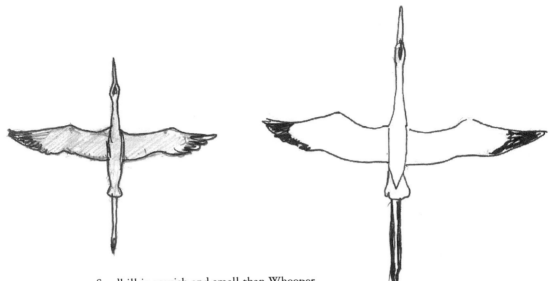

Sandhill is grayish and small than Whooper.
The Whooper is white with black wingtips.

times to a single north/south line in spring up through the Central Plains — Oklahoma, Kansas, Nebraska where they paused at the Platte River then flew northward over the Dakotas toward the Canadian border to vanish, literally vanish somewhere in the far unknown reaches of the Canadian wilderness. There they bred and nested, and in the fall returned to South Texas. But these breeding grounds were yet not located when Allen began his investigation. They remained as mysterious as ever when he published his comprehensive monograph *The Whooping Crane Research Report* in 1952.

To write an extensive "life history" of any bird, as Allen had already written with *The Roseate Spoonbill, Research Report No. 2*, also published by the Audubon Society, requires a prodigious amount of time and patient observation in the field. Aware that he, along with other scientists, knew very little of the Whooping Crane's behavior in the wild — or even in captivity for that matter — Allen was mindful of the necessity to observe the wild birds at close hand. But to observe a wild Whooping Crane by getting close enough to monitor its wild traits, Allen knew would be difficult, yet not a total impossibility.

One major trait, however, of the Crane family — any of the fifteen species — always mentioned by any observer from Aristotle to Audubon, is the unvarying comment on the bird's wariness, its ability to hide in the reeds or to escape at the faintest crack of twig or rustle of marsh grass. This, at least, was known to all. Everyone who had ever seen a Whooping Crane learned (to use novelist Muriel Sparks' words) that the "lightest footfall was taken with fanatical seriousness" by the white birds.

This particular behavioral trait made the Trumpeter Swan and the cautious Whooping Crane a "shining mark for every hunter with a gun" according to ornithologist Edward Howe Forbush. Thus, in the 1890s to bag the Whooping Crane was a challenge far greater than to bag the more populous Sandhill Crane. The Whooping Crane was a "trophy bird," not only singled out as a rarity but passionately stalked by hunters who took them from the skies with guns or by hunter-collectors who took eggs from their nests with their bare hands.

If you exclude subsistence hunters, the early hunters here were first the commercial hunters, followed by sport hunters. But, if the market hunters wanted to boast of their accomplishments in taking the white Cranes, they did not profusely write of it. However, "sport hunting" literature, handed down to Americans from the English, was a popular genre in the 1800s as it still is today. There can be no doubt that an eyewitness account has a vivid intensity about it.

One illustrious sport writer Theodore S. Van Dyke in his *Game Birds at Home* (1895) draws a clear picture of his heated search and desperate longing to kill a Whooping Crane. His account was authentic and reliable enough to be part of Allen's later "Kill Records."

Van Dyke tells how he deliberately passed up the easier Sandhills flocking in his gun sights while he hunted the Bolson de Mapini, a tableland of Northern Mexico, and an area, no doubt, near where ornithologist Henry Dresser reported them thirty years earlier. When Van Dyke came across the white birds foraging in the cornfields, he listened to their calls which sounded to him like the "blast of a silverhorn." He stood up and swung his shotgun at the first white Crane which "clawed the air barely thirty feet away." (Van Dyke quoted by Doughty).

Like a child stealing an egg from an anxious mother-Robin's nest, the mature hunter has mixed emotions, when he admits to his readers that "it seemed wicked to spoil anything so rare and beautiful as that sight!"

But the hunter's zeal for the "shot of a lifetime," a magnificent trophy-bird, overcomes any hesitation he might have in destroying this "rare and beautiful bird"; consequently, his first shot "caught the Crane midflight — and it plunged earthward. The second cut down its mate in a revolving whirl of black and carmine." Thus, this very accurate marksman had with only two blasts killed a mated pair, causing them, as he puts it rather exultantly, "to relax their hold on the warm sunlight."

Bovus Absurdus: The Canvas Beast

Like Theodore Van Dyke fifty years before him, Robert Porter Allen was a hunter for the trophy bird. But his passionate desire for the white Crane was a distinctly different kind. Born the year of the Audubon Society's founding in 1905 "for the protection of birds," Allen, the first Audubon Research Director, was a new breed of avian scientist with a new consciousness. Unlike most of his predecessors in the 1800s and early 1900s, he did not "take live specimens" to study the dead skins. Rather he felt the need to observe the bird behavior in their actual habitat.

To seek and to find the Roseate Spoonbill by avoiding an alligator or two, he slogged through Florida tropical swamps and Texas wetlands. Now, at Aransas, with its vast open reaches of saltmarsh, its great uninterrupted vistas of landscape where an upright human was a formidable sight to a Crane, observing Cranes in their own territory without disturbing them took not only a clever and ingenious plan, but a certain knowledge of the ways of this ever cautious bird.

Allen noticed that the Cranes passed quite near cattle — totally heedless of them and without the slightest signs of wariness — just as I had seen the Sandhills, heedless of the Santa Gertrudis cattle at the King Ranch.

Therefore, he constructed a giant canvas blind painted mahogany red in the shape of a Santa Gertrudis — cow or bull. (Gender will matter as you will see farther on.) With this ingenious and lightweight moveable blind or "hide" as the English call it, he could spend hours inside his "canvas beast" engaged in the close observation of the nonchalant Whoopers.

Roseate Spoonbill.

The first day Allen hid in his bull/blind, he spent so long in wait that he fell asleep. But he was suddenly startled into wakefulness by the "clear Ker-lee-oo of a Crane." He spied two adult Cranes far to the west, but after a while "with more whoops, the two birds disappeared."

As Allen's narrative unravels, the good-natured wit and humor of the man become apparent. For, serious of purpose though he was on the "Trail of Vanishing Birds," he had the ability to look at the bizarre side of the torturous hours in the field with the grace and levity of a master story-teller, and he was unafraid to poke fun at himself.

"The next day," Allen tells us, after his first fruitless day in the blind, he was back again inside his "canvas beast" to which he had by now given the classification in Latin of "absurd bull" — *Bovus absurdus*. Again he waited, hour upon hour, with all the patience of a Carancahua brave hidden in the reeds, longbow at the ready.

But, rather than sighting a white Crane, he saw to his horror another animal straying near the blind, a Santa Gertrudis, began to hunker nearby. "It was a live bull, and a red one at that!" Allen says. "His head was lifted, as he was trying to catch my scent. I stood perfectly still and stared into his uncharitable eyes, scarcely breathing and unwilling to look away for fear he might charge ... It was only 10 A.M. at the time. I was composing headlines BIRD WATCHER GORED BY BULL and so on, when my silent adversary suddenly turned and walked away. His expression now appeared to be one of complete boredom."

Allen would make use of his canvas bull again — but that time it would be a world famous *Life* magazine photographer inside the red monster, and the photographer would succeed in his photo-quest, thus putting the Whooping Crane's image into the memory bank of thousands and thousands of Americans who had no idea how a Whooping Crane looked.

Record High

The image of Robert Porter Allen inside a canvas beast and peering through its snout is fresh in my mind when I set out from Corpus Christi for Aransas National Wildlife Refuge straight northward on Highway 35.

A gray day mid-January. This morning over breakfast, I read the headlines in the *Corpus Christi Caller-Times*: "Whooping Cranes at Record High!" Tom Stehn, Wildlife Biologist of Aransas Refuge, who today, like Allen fifty years ago, doesn't spare himself in keeping track of the Whooping Crane population has counted at least one hundred fifty-six in his aerial survey once every week. It's a "conservative estimate," for the count may be as high as one hundred fifty-seven or eight. But Cranes may "fly across the bays and be counted twice." (By the Spring of 2000, Tom Stehn will count 187 Whoopers starting out migration.)

Of course this year's record high is good news. But the members of the Whooping Crane Recovery Team, which Stehn co-chairs with Canadian Brian Johns, are as wary about the Whooping Crane's survival as the cautious bird upon which they center their energies. A natural disaster such as a hurricane making landfall on this coast, as it has more than once — tearing away shoreline, uprooting the ornamental palm trees and the strong native trees as well, tumbling houses and snapping boats into kindling — also devastates the area wildlife. Thus, natural or manmade disasters such as oil spills have the potential to wipe out most of the entire flock. The threat is ever-present.

Just to be on the safe side, biologists have established another flock of feral Cranes: Whooping Cranes reared in captivity and released into the wild. This flock in Florida is overseen by Stephen Nesbitt. He has achieved some success with the white Cranes released in the Kissimmee Prairie area,

A careful, disciplined, and holistic approach is necessary to the conservation of Crane habitats in order to help preserve them. Eleven of the 15 species of Cranes are near extinction, making Cranes one of the most threatened families of birds in the world.

the traditional residence of the Florida Sandhill Crane. One of the six sub-species or races of Sandhills, the Gray Crane has its own Latin descriptive name *Grus canadensis pratensis*. The name, credited in 1794 to F.A. Meyer, is a Latin reference to its savannah, open prairie-like habitat, for indeed the Florida Sandhill remains all year in the Florida savannahs and nests there.

In colonial times, and some claim later, the Whooping Crane was also present, known by the native American tribes, and seen by America's first native-born naturalist of European stock William Bartram. Bartram gave it the descriptive name *Grus clamator* — literally shouting or clamoring Crane. The Whooper's bones have been found in Florida dating back to the Pleistocene epoch " near Melbourne and Seminole, Florida."

As I near the turnoff to Aransas Wildlife Refuge, seeing evidence of a controlled burn-off, I catch sight of grassfires, a straight line of yellow tongues. White smoke rolls like a giant cornucopia into the gray Texas sky. I pass long stretches of flat land where the burn-off has already taken place, possibly a month ago. New winter grass shows plainly among the blackened twigs. Prescribed burn-off is a comparatively new-found concept of setting a fire to renew the earth — to renew and not to destroy, a concept inherited from the natural lightning strikes since time before time. The Whoopers benefit from the prescribed burn offs, according to Tom Stehn, because the Oak/brush lands may present a natural barrier to their choice feeding on acorns. The grass is too tall for even this lanky five-foot tall bird to dine on acorns. The birds will enter a burned off field and easily select the acorns, which have fallen from the trees, sometimes nicely roasted.

Finally I see the rough brown sign with white letters and a flying white goose announcing the turn-off to the Refuge. At Refuge headquarters, a low modern building, I walk past a sign informing me to "Bee Aware of Killer Bees!" The volunteer at the desk signs me in. A woman in her late sixties or so, she wears a pin announcing she has "devoted over 1000 volunteer hours". She tells me that some volunteers "come down here with family and trailers and stay all winter right here at the Refuge." Then, smiling with the crinkly look around the eyes folks around here get from staring at birds in the Texas sun, she hands me a map of the Refuge.

For a moment, I envy her and want to trade lives with her, this "1000 hour volunteer." I envy her for her service to Cranes and for her

Detail of Algonquin petroglyph near Peterborough, Ontario— Northern Woodland *(redrawn from a photograph by K. Wellmann in* Rock Art of the American Indian*)*.

living here all winter, easily among the Cranes, knowing where they are today, where they will be tomorrow, watching them at dawn in "first light" or at dusk when the sea and the world seem to slow down.

But I look at the brochure and get the facts: 54,829 acres operated by the U.S. Fish and Wildlife Service since 1937, a dog-ear shaped peninsula protected by the low-lying Matagorda Island where "strong winds push the bay waters over low-lying shores, forming tidal marshes among the short salt-tolerant vegetation. Mild winters and abundant food supplies attract over 289 species including Egrets, Spoonbills, Ducks and Geese". (USFWS). But in winter from October to March, the chance to see the rare Whooping Cranes in the wild attracts myriads of visitors from all over the U.S. and the world. Because it's cloudy today, visitors are sparse. When I ask where a good place would be today to spot Whooping Cranes she tells me, "Heron Flats — but don't take your dog with you — alligators and killer bees are around too."

Alone, I find the pathway through gnarled black-jack oaks — the kind naturalist Jean Berlandier must have found when he put ashore in 1829. It's a good twisting walk, the path as gnarled as the oaks. Occasional sunlight barely filters through in pale light spangles dappling the wood. Now, I'm out of the trees and on a path through prairie grass, its tiers of color marking the contour of the slope: winter-browned Bluestem, and then, the Marsh Grass of green to the water. On my left is a deep ditch of fresh water, but I see no Alligator as I have in the past. Once, several years ago, I rounded this same turn and came upon a huddle of humans, one armed with a camera equipped with a long-range lens angled downward on its tripod to photograph a Texas Alligator close up. It looked up at the group with that wily and toothy amphibian half-smile, mischevious and knowing.

The sandy path loops upward over a dune, and as I top it I inhale the smell of the sea and come in sight of the Whooping Cranes, a pair feeding in the shallows of the Heron Flats inlet — precisely the way the "1000 hour volunteer" told me they would be.

The sight of them makes me stop to gaze at them, these tall, mighty, yet fragile creatures: unaware of me and busily occupied. They step with care in their sedate gravitas, such a large and long-legged bird, one which seems to prefer to walk than take wing, in its constant search for clams, crabs and all the delectable twenty-seven or so species of "critters" tasty enough to entice the Whoopers on their arduous three thousand mile flight to this semi-tropical protection near the sea, far from their isolated breeding grounds in Canada's interior Northwest Territories high up near the Arctic Circle.

Part loosely wing
the region,
part more wise
In common range
in figure,
wedge their way,
Intelligent of seasons,
and set forth
Their aery caravan
high over seas
Flying and over lands
with mutual wing
Easing their flight.
So steers
the prudent crane
Her annual voyage,
borne on winds;
the air
Floats as they pass,
fanned with
unnumbered plumes

JOHN MILTON

It is a moment of silent privilege, I feel. A private wonder, a miracle of nature that could make everyone who ever searched the horizon or sky for bird, pause and plant their feet in absolute reverence. Rare birds of time, the ancient past and hopefully future millennia. The sight of them links me as one inextricably bound and at one with all life on this self-renewing planet as it loops around its star — our sun — now only beginning to show through the mist to illumine the bare flesh of their red crowns and the gentle curve of their white, white feathers.

An hour passes without my noticing it, and, with my skin yet unwelted by Killer Bee attack, I go safely down the sandy hill retracing my steps on the twisted path. Nearing the ditch of water I see the Alligator. It has appeared from wherever it lurked in the marsh. We exchange meaningful sidelong glances. Each is prepared to ignore the other. But my hand goes almost automatically to the camera slung over one shoulder. Then I remember my supply is exhausted from taking three rolls of the Whooping Cranes. But this "photogenic" American Alligator, so elegant in its great scaly length, would probably prefer the quietude of its amphibian world without the click of a shutter.

The three rolls of exposed film snug in my pocket, I think how much the camera gives me in a search for wildlife — particularly rare birds afield. It is an instrument enabling me to seize the moment, giving me a kind of steady present.

At home in the more wintery north with only a swarm of Sparrows and a single House Finch to gaze at through the windows, I may study the behavior of the wild Cranes and recapture the nuances of ever changing light and movement. No matter how carefully I compose the picture in the heat of the moment, each freshly developed and printed roll unfolds endless surprises.

The great French photographer Henri Cartier-Bresson called the instant a shutter clicks, the "decisive moment." And what I look for in that critical instant of decision is the extraordinary gesture of each rare bird, a biography of light, shadow and form; an impression of the Crane from which an image emerges, not just from the rolls of film, but a picture I carry away in my own eyes and heart, the imprint of a life moment — the bird's and mine.

Sun-Writing

At the "decisive moment" in the history of photography of the world's first photo, the camera didn't click. One moment in 1826, a new technology was invented, eventually serving to record this planet or the rocks on Mars: a simple pewter plate coated with bitumen was soundlessly exposed to light.

Thus the first photographer with the mellifluous sounding French name of Nicephore Niepce created what he called a "heliograph" — literally a "sun-writing," from the Greek "helio" = sun and "graph" = writing. Niepce's first photograph was astonishing. In one instant he was able to fix "permanently the image of nature" on a metal plate through the action of sunlight. He exposed the plate and later washed it "with a mixture of oils which dissolved away the parts of bitumen by light" (Gersheim quoting Niepce).

Niepce was exploring this marvelous technology just about the same time another Frenchman, Jean James Audubon was in Louisiana creating an image by hand, executing a drawing of a Whooping Crane about to devour a baby Alligator, the same food the extinct Carancahua Indians ate. Audubon's depiction of *The Birds of America* would be the first time many people caught sight of a Whooping Crane's image.

What, you might ask, does photography have to do with the Whooping Crane and Robert Porter Allen? The answer is that to Allen, photography was of great

Whooping Crane by John James Audubon.

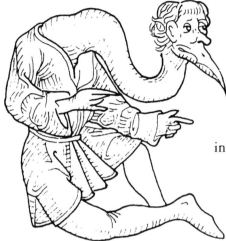

importance, a major technology available to him for studying the Crane and for putting the image of this rare Crane before the eyes of Americans everywhere. He particularly wanted his target group, the hunters living along the Central Plains flyway, who frequently mistook the great white Crane for everything from the much smaller Snow Goose to the White Pelican to see it. One Great Whooping Crane had languished for quite a time in captivity at a Gun Club in Nebraska, mistaken for a Heron, thus, one single photograph would bring the Whooping Crane out of the mystery of the past and put it into the minds and hearts of Americans. Allen was to achieve this miracle by employing his "canvas beast" as a blind and enclosing a world famous photographer inside it.

AGRIPPPINI— In the folk-tale of Duke Ernst, a people in human form, but with pointed beaks. Also called Crane Heads. *Glossary of Monsters*

Everything "fell into place" for Allen when he received a phone call from a *Life* editor. The editor/friend was sending a staff photographer, Andreas Feininger, son of the famous Cubist artist Lyonel Feininger. Andreas, Lyonel's oldest son, was an accomplished photojournalist and photographic artist in his own right. Not only would the result be the serious purpose of getting the Whooping Crane on film, but again, Allen's sense of humor will enter into his story, his account giving us one of the most entertaining narratives in the history of wildlife photography.

When Andreas Feininger arrived, it took an "operation" on the bull/blind's nostril to fit his "two big lenses into the head of the beast." Allen knew that, Andreas, a New Yorker suddenly thrust into the heart of the wintery Texas wilderness marsh, would find the long wait inside the blind a miserable experience, so he went to great lengths to make Feininger comfortable, even finding a "canvas stool" for the photographer to sit on. Two days went by "without a Whooping Crane in sight." Or, if they did appear, it was too foggy for photography.

A third day and the fog cleared off: "Andreas settled in the blind with his equipment including some sandwiches and a jug of water." Then Allen, of all people, interrupts his narrative to appreciate a trait in Feininger which so many people found in Allen himself, and observes that Andreas "was certainly determined."

Allen spent part of the third day watching from a "safe distance": "the South Family appeared, taking a stand directly south of camp and about a half mile beyond Andreas." However, just at this moment, Allen was called away to tend to some other business and was delayed. He worried that Andreas would be "chased all over the marsh by a real bull." But Andreas was "safe and sound" on Allen's return. After nine hours in the blind, he had never seen a Whooping Crane.

"The next morning," Allen says," it was do or die." As he and Feininger were moving the blind to what they thought might be a "more favorable spot, the South Family group saw us and started calling." Allen dropped to the ground and crawled away on his belly. "However, with no apparent suspicion of Bovus absurdus, the Whoopers came right on, and a short while later trooped past Andreas in single file."

At last, the "decisive moment" came, and Feininger took his photograph, a single shot in very poor light conditions at one thousand feet, but it was good enough to appear in the *Life* issue of March 3, 1947, an issue in which Cartier-Bresson's famous photograph of an anonymous man jumping over a puddle appeared, and also Edwin Land introduced his "Land Polaroid" camera.

But Allen, knowing how difficult it was to get this breakthrough photographic image, observes that Feininger, "the very best of photographers probably didn't think much of it, but it was one of the few pictures we have of a family of Whooping Cranes striding across the marsh sounding their magnificent call." *(Vanishing Birds)*.

Late in the spring I visited a friend in Sechuan Province. A pair of cranes danced in a clear stream. I observed their feathers white as snow, and the top of their heads red like vermillion. They fluttered up and down, and took their bath while dancing. Then they spread their wings and flew high in the sky and cried in harmony in the azure vault, making me feel without doubt that they were immortals.

TIEN-WEN-KO
CH'IN-PU-CHI-CHENG
Introduction to Lute Music
(a Ming Dynasty handbook).

Remembering the Territory

The sun's out. In its warmth, a few bees laze around my head. As I reach the Ford Explorer parked at the entrance to Heron Flats path, I slip in beneath the steering wheel and gaze at them through rolled up windows. They are native bees — not "killers," and I jot this fact down in my field notes along with, of course, the sighting of the Whooping Crane pair.

Luckily there are reinforcements for my photo-taking passion. Five fresh rolls in my camera bag and I'm ready to go to the Observation Tower just a few miles along the Refuge road. There, armed with film and long-range lens, I feel secure that I'll see more Whoopers and get a photo. I say this, for I've been coming to Aransas over a score of years, and I have never failed to see Whooping Cranes from the Observation Tower overlooking the wide curve of the estuary and marshland.

Interestingly enough, Robert Porter Allen observed that the white Cranes returned each year to the same territory in Aransas, not in flocks as does the Sandhill, but in family groups, a tradition which the first USFWS Director Stevenson had also noted.

When I pass along the road which now opens up to my left a view of the Gulf comes into sight, the horizon broken only by the low horizontal shape of Matagorda Island and the vertical upright of a Great Blue Heron fishing on the near shore. To my right, a Peregrine Falcon settles at the top of a tree in the motte of oaks.

At King Ranch, I saw three Peregrine Falcons (*Falco peregrinis*), literally, "traveling" falcon. The presence of these handsome small raptors, sometimes called "Duck Hawks" is an avian imprint on conservation's pages, comparable in some ways to the Whoopers' "record high" population here at Aransas. Like the Whooping Crane's survival, the Falcon's also started with a captive breeding program. But the Falcon's was far more recent than the Whooper's.

Consisting of a complex, but precise, duet, the unison call is performed by a pair of mated Cranes. Females have a two-note call while males have a single-note call. The pair usually stand within a few feet of each other while calling.

By 1960, "the entire population of Peregrine Falcons disappeared from the east," according to biologists Anne and Paul Erlich in *Extinction.* "Feeding at the top of the food chain, the Falcons were endangered by build-up of chlorinated hydrocarbons such as DDT [the same problem attributed to the decline of the Eagle population]."

Ornithologist "Tom Cade of Cornell University attempted to arrest the decline of the population." Like Allen, "Cade persisted in the face of great difficulties." Starting in 1970, "breeding success in captivity was not achieved until three years later, when twenty eggs hatched .... By 1979, the first four chicks were hatched in the wild."

And here I am, twenty years later, one birdwatcher lucky enough to spot, in the short space of two days, a total of four Peregrines, this one with its dark high shouldered silhouette on a Blackjack Oak tree at Aransas.

If Jean Berlandier saw them in 1829, he would have called them "faucon gentil" — French for "noble falcon" because of the bird's adeptness in falconry, the hunting sport of nobles and kings since the Crusaders brought it back from the Middle East.

Eagles may be a threat to Cranes, particularly in nesting season, but because of their small size — no bigger than a Crow, Peregrine Falcons, speedy raptors though they are, probably do not pose a threat to Whoopers or Sandhills. There is much folk wisdom in the Spanish proverb quoted by Gabriel Garcia Marquez: "A Falcon who chases a warlike Crane can only hope for a life of pain."

Grazing beneath the watchful eye of the Falcon, is a family of White-tailed Deer, also the King's favorite game, a native ungulate and peaceful grass-eater neither threatened nor endangered.

When this area of Blackjack Peninsula was purchased by the Government on the establishment of the Refuge, it was known as the "St. Charles Ranch," a ranch owned by Attorney Leroy G. Denham. He turned a working ranch into a kind of fantastic wildlife park, releasing exotic animals, mammals, and birds onto this sparse hostile area. Among the mammals were Fallow Deer (*Cervus dama*, a small European deer), not to mention numerous species of exotic birds. Fortunately, for this land, most did not survive in this alien biome. When the Fallow Deer succumbed, the White-tailed native Deer filled the niche, taking over in great numbers.

The White-tailed Deer, with very few predators to encounter, proliferated, their numbers growing to enormous proportions and creating no doubt a dismal situation at Aransas — a situation which may happen with even a native species when its numbers grow to astronomical pro-

In Germany a Falcon or a small Eagle and in Tartary a Gyrfalcon is taught to fly at Cranes and Swans; therefore, the Germans call such a Hawk a Crane-Hawk or Gyrfalcon.

REV. EDWARD TOPSELL

portions. When this occurs, the native species' great number threatens its own survival by its very success at surviving. Biologists are on the alert to overpopulation, and they take steps in wildlife management to thin the populations — unlike *Homo sapiens*, a species which is probably the most successful mammalian species of all in spreading its population all over the planet.

Consequently, with the White-tailed Deer overpowering the Peninsula, the first Aransas Director James Osborne Stevenson rounded up over thirteen thousand five hundred White-tails. With conservation of natural creatures on the minds of far-sighted biologists, the deer were not slaughtered as "pests," a traditional procedure, but they served, according to Robin Doughty, "as seed stock for the Texas Hill Country," that scenic area west of Austin which is craggy, wooded, and beautiful unlike the rest of the plains of Texas.

Stevenson always felt the Whooping Crane to be his "centerpiece" in the rich wild life of Aransas and the reason for the establishment of

Illustration for a Russian fairy tale showing a curious Eurasian Crane.

the Refuge in 1937. And it was Stevenson who made the first "official headcount of the Whoopers in 1938 which he set at eighteen Whoopers in all: fourteen adults and four sub-adults."

Furthermore, Stevenson first noted how the Whooping Cranes were such staunch holders of a territory at the Refuge. When Allen arrived, almost ten years after him, he built on Stevenson's observations extending them by his careful immersion into the life and traits of the Whoopers. By studying a captive breeding pair, he estimated the pair held a territory "one mile in length by more than a quarter mile in width."

If you begin to cross over into the paradox of nature as I am here, you know when you make one observation about a creature in nature as an absolute fact, you're entering quicksand, for, on further study, you are soon proved wrong by this creature. But there is one rule I will dare to make concerning Whooping Crane behavior: they will return to the same territory, with the same partner, year after year (perhaps).

Yet, as Robin Doughty says, "a pair or family group may leave its chosen habitat from time to time as events and opportunities dictate: it also may enlarge its proprietary space if owner of adjacent territories fails to show up. But it is faithful to a specific locality."

In his *Research Report*, Allen charted the Whooping Crane Territory, and his map which folds out of the Research book gives you a roadmap from the Crane's eye view of the length and breadth of each territory, and holds fairly true today. (Please note, the statement is qualified with "fairly.")

Tom Stehn with naturalist Frank Johnson combined data from Allen, primarily, but others too, and made a more recent aerial census to determine the number, location, and size of Whooping Crane territories. They found that Allen's territorial map held up for a long time. He had calculated that the average territory was four hundred twenty-five acres. Twenty-five years later, Dave Blankenship, an Audubon staff biologist like Allen, found his own average agreed with Allen's earlier calculation. But when Tom Stehn made his calculations ten years after that, he discovered there had been quite a change in the size of the territory: it had fallen by almost a third to two hundred eighty-nine acres. (Doughty).

The diminishing territory is a consequence occurring rather naturally. Young birds — rejected by their parents after a first winter of slavish and devotedly attentive care — will stake out territory near where they spent their first winter with their parents. Yes, Whooping Cranes, unlike Thomas Wolfe's humans "can go home again."

I round a curve and come in sight of the Observation Tower, a cement square aloft against the sky like a crow's nest of a tall ship. At first glance it seems to rise as if it were lifted up by an umbrella of leaves in the Live Oaks surrounding and hiding its ramp and supports.

Parking, I get out to walk over by the sign bearing a life size image of a Whooping Crane pair. I always make it a ritual to stop before the sign and read it, a ritual which I always perform because the written message is clear and meaningful — meaningful for all of the effort it took naturalists such as Robert Porter Allen and now Tom Stehn to study Crane habits long enough to be able to sum up hours of field work into this information:

EACH WHOOPING CRANE FAMILY OCCUPIES A LARGE AREA OR TERRITORY DURING THEIR STAY ON THE REFUGE. THE FAMILY DEFENDS THIS HOME GROUND FROM THE INTRUSION OF OTHER WHOOPING CRANES. THE EXPANSE OF GRASSY FLATS SEEN FROM THIS TOWER IS USUALLY PART OF THE TERRITORY OF JUST ONE FAMILY OF CRANES.

The Observation Tower rises high at Aransas National Wildlife Refuge near Corpus Christi, Texas. This 54,829 acre refuge occupies the Blackjack Peninsula, named for its scattered blackjack oaks. Grasslands, live oaks and red bay thickets grow in deep, sandy soils. Inland, the water changes from salty flats to freshwater ponds. This habitat attracts over 389 bird species, including pelicans, egrets, spoonbills, ducks and geese.

I mount the zig-zag ramp, walking to and fro like a tracker dog as I make my ascent upward through the motte of thick-leaved Oaks to finally reach the platform overlooking the wide expanse of sea and marsh grass.

The day is clear now, and the clouds seem to sail like a flock of Snow Geese overhead. Far, far away in all that immense green I make out the distinctive white shapes of the Crane family moving through the grass. But there is something else I see. A pair emerges from the grass and makes an investigative tour along the yellow-brown sandy area intersected by silvery flat swirls of water issuing from a hummock of land and grass.

Through the telescope available for Aransas visitors, I make out two more Cranes with a young one. Five in all. But a line has been "drawn in the sand." A definite borderline, for, the two Crane families pass up and down, up and down, feeding casually as if there were an invisible but impenetrable Berlin Wall between each pair. No Crane puts a foot over the other's borderline, and their advance and retreat is synchronized right up and down a line marking the frontier of a pair's chosen land.

A score of years ago when coming for the first time, I was so awed I made field notes on the experience, never thinking to put them to use. That day was also a winter day, and the population of Whooping Cranes calculated then at ninety-one in all. The statistic included those in captive programs as well as this single wild group.

That particular Aransas winter, the wild population numbered at total of seventy-eight birds, seventy-two adults and six young. Less than half of today's number. But not, I thought at the time, looking out at the pair, anything to celebrate. I had just seen some new statistics on human populations, and we were definitely multiplying — the world population of Homo sapiens had tripled since my first birthday. As Allen says of "us" and the Whoopers: "The human population curve rises as theirs falls."

When I look at my notes from twenty years ago, the words seem to be a conduit to today's experience. I write my reactions: "When I put my eye to the scope, and the pair comes into focus, I feel as if I am tunnelling into the beginnings of the world. On the day we named them with their own call, our new word flew away from us on great white wings. Now, I see before me the details of a new vision, a new definition of reality, but a sight which is ancient as the beginning of time."

There can be no doubt that the Whooping Crane with its primordial aspect is worthy of commanding our respect. And a line of biologists like Robert Porter Allen, a half century ago, and Tom Stehn today, have indeed done humankind a service in their diligence and perseverance to restore and work towards the survival of the rare and mighty species of the tallest of North American birds — and certainly excepting those birds such as the Attwater's Prairie Chicken, some of which may be sighted here at Aransas, a bird almost as "scarce as hen's teeth" numbering only fifty in all, the Whooping Crane still remains endangered.

The Chinese character for "Crane" — "he" (Pinyin) or "ho" (Wade-Giles). Using 21 strokes, it is a combination of "soaring" (or "heading off into the distance") and "bird with long feathers." As Ernest Fenellosa remarked, the visual quality of Chinese ideograms "carry within them the verbal idea of action."

Reading the Code: From Egg to Adult

With the Whooping Cranes my only subject, I've taken three more rolls of film. But I know from experience that even a fairly high-powered lens will give me mostly a vista of green salt marsh, gray Gulf, and tawny sand dotted here and there with the distant shapes of the white-feathered and imperious Cranes.

Although the Cranes will appear minuscule in the rectangle of the photo, the distinctive shape of Crane will define the landscape. They will appear as white and shining marks set in green, and easily recognizable.

This recognition of distant Cranes comes from long hours of watching them — far distant and undisturbed birds here in Texas, and marvelously close-up — near enough to fill the lens — in Wisconsin's International Crane Foundation.

Although he had his fellow team members of the US Fish and Wildlife Service biologists, in those days, Robert Porter Allen did not have a corps of "seasoned Crane watchers" such as the "1,000-hour volunteer" to draw upon as he studied their habits and traits. That circumstance alone fifty years ago made the *Life* magazine photo an important tool to get out the message of the image of the Whooping Crane's appearance.

In the same spring of 1947 when the photo appeared, and after the Whoopers left on migration from Aransas toward the "unknown land" of Canada which Allen called "terra incognita," he followed them northward along the thin line of their flyway up through

Productive tidal flats of Aransas National Wildlife Refuge provide clams and crabs for the Whoopers to eat.

Texas, western Oklahoma, Kansas, and Nebraska. In Nebraska, he stopped at the Platte River, the same pause the Whoopers and Sandhills make on their journeys. By the end of March, however, generally most of the Sandhills leave the Platte for their far-flung nesting territories. The Whoopers arrive in April in Nebraska, traveling not in the great flocks as the Sandhills do but in small family groups, three or four birds at a time. Thus, in April, on the braided river, Allen himself succeeded in photographing five migrating Whoopers. But as he says in the caption of the photo, "It took a great deal of luck to get this photograph of five migrant Whooping Cranes on a sandbar in the Platte River in Nebraska."

First of all, he had to rent an airplane: the five, possibly two family units, are pictured from an aerial perspective, a cluster as small — but not quite — as my own photos of them taken from the tower in Aransas. The five are clearly defined shapes of white against the darker river sand. Allen might have captured the Whoopers on film, but like all the other migrating white Cranes, a grand total of twenty-five adults, six young that year, the five too, vanished over the Canadian border, flying into terra incognita. He went on to Canada — but no luck. The Cranes had vanished across the borders of human knowledge.

The map of Canada, stretching as it does east and west along the boundary of the U.S. and plunging northward into the Arctic was as blank to the Crane biologists as if it had never been explored by the early Europeans of the 1600s and 1700s. Even Allen's colleague Fred Bard in Saskatchewan could not pinpoint the Crane's whereabouts. No one alive could.

Allen knew that if they did not find the Whooping Crane's nesting area there would be no way for the Canadian Wildlife biologists to protect them or for a study to be made of their "Life History" from egg to adult. The reason, of course, is that the Whoopers Allen and the team could observe were wintering Cranes which had gone by the time they would mate and nest.

There was one answer and one only: to breed a pair of Cranes in captivity and to rear them in Aransas.

Pairing wild creatures in a captive and controlled situation has been — and still is — a procedure which stirs up a debate among life-scientists. Sometimes the debate grows fervent. Absolute purists on the side of "wildness" state emphatically that humankind should "not interfere with nature." They are wholeheartedly against any taint of the human hand extended into nature's realm.

Cranes are the stuff of magic, whose voices penetrate the atmosphere of the world's wilderness areas.

PAUL JOHNSGARD,
Crane Music

The contingent on the other side in favor of captive breeding, particularly endangered species, reason that human beings have interfered with nature to such an extent that our very existence has degraded the environment. From the primal hunter driving a spear into the side of a Mammoth to the modern motorist driving a mammoth car, its tailpipe spewing hydrocarbons into the atmosphere, our very civilized existence, they say, has imperiled so many species that there "must be human interference to save the wild species and to restore them to their habitat."

In all its complexity, ever-changing nature has not yielded up definitive answers to the debate — so far. But, as it turns out, time did reveal a partial answer to the complex argument, one which might only be viewed in retrospect. That answer is glimpsed down the corridor of fifty years. Yet, it turns out, each side — wildness versus captive breeding of Whooping Cranes — may claim partial success.

However, the partial solution to their argument did not come without enormous human effort on the part of the corps of avian naturalists who, with the vast intricacies of trial and error, learned to accept "no" as positive an answer as "yes" when it comes to the intense experiments within nature's realm. This answer however would not be given up even partially until the Whooping Crane's breeding area was found.

Allen could not wait. He knew that he must learn all he could about the Whooper's nesting habits and rearing their young even before they were found in Canada.

Thus, he embarked on his own plan which followed a path right through the center of the controversy.

Flexible as nature itself, apparently Allen could always find a solution to a knotty problem. He had a solution for this one. And an ethical one at that, for he believed wholeheartedly along with the rest of the Audubon Society in wildness. He would breed a pair of adult birds, defective ones such as one with a broken wing.

Yet he needed birds which could be reasonably expected to be able to produce young. Adult birds would be used because there was no way to rear a Whooping Crane from the egg. This was out of the question. The "last nest" of Whoopers had been found in Canada by Gameskeeper Fred Bradshaw in 1922, a quarter of a century before Allen even thought of rearing a white Crane.

Bradshaw had fortunately taken a photo of the Whooper's nest, and the photo was a rare one, a prize appearing in *Life-Histories of American Marsh Birds* by distinguished ornithologist A.C. Bent in 1926. Bradshaw's photo and Bent's information gave questioning humans an inkling of where the Whoopers nested. The great Arthur Cleveland Bent who had cast an eye on many a marsh bird had to admit he had never seen the Whooper's "downy young." Nor, of course, had Allen fifty years later.

But Allen began at the beginning by close observation of the wintering Cranes' behavior. He writes: "Today the first signs of a new breeding cycle are observed on the Texas coast. At the start, only one bird of a pair is seen leaping into the air, springing several feet off the ground, wings flapping."

Spring came, the summer passed, and in the fall the Whoopers returned. Allen was out in the field and continuing his observation: "A brief but complete dance was seen on January 26. Suddenly one bird (the male?) began bowing his head and flapping his wings. At the same time he leaped stiffly into the air, an amazing bounce on stiffened legs that carried him nearly three feet off the ground. In the air he threw his head back so that the bill pointed skyward, neck arched over his back. Throughout the leap the great wings were constantly flapping their long black flight feather in striking contrast to the dazzling white of the rest of the plumage.

"The second bird (the female?) was facing the first individual when he reached the ground after completing the initial bounce. This second bird ran forward a few steps, pumping her head up and down, flapping her wings. Then both birds leaped into the air, wings flapping, neck doubled up over their backs, legs thrust downward stiffly."

Allen accompanied these passages describing the Crane Dance with handsome drawings of the dancing Whoopers. The gesture of the great white bird is there to see and to read. It is a visual and verbal biography of one instant snipped from lengthy hours of observation.

One hundred years before Allen watched the Aransas dancers, naturalist/writer Henry David Thoreau noted in his journal an axiom which anyone making an observation in words or drawings and photographs of animals could use to this day. Thoreau made use of the more literary term "biography" rather than the natural scientist's "life history" but the axiom is clear for any naturalist to follow.

Thoreau points out: "If you have undertaken to write the biography of an animal, you will have to present the living creature [that is] a result which no man can understand, but only in his degree report the impression made on him."

Clearly, Allen grasped the impression of the dance. Any observer would see the dance as a flourish of feathers, riffling past his eyes at electronic speed. Yet Allen could also reproduce the movement — almost as accurately as a digital camera in the hands of a wildlife photographer. But Allen somehow or other managed to reduce the motion to a slow speed, letting us see each of its rapid components, framing the gestures with remarkably apt and wondrous care.

The language in Allen's Whooping Crane dance passage in his Research Report also reveals another important fact. His questions — "(the male?)" and "(the female?)" — treating with the sex of the two dancers show the lack of prevailing knowledge of gender among scientists.

It would take another naturalist who also both literally and figuratively immersed himself in the life of a Whooper by actually living and dancing with a single female Crane, who just arrived in the world about the time Allen writes his observations. George Archibald would come up with the answer in determining the sex of each Crane by observation. The ritual dance and the Cranes' shared call, "the unison call," gave Archibald the answer. That scientist, Archibald, founder with Ron Sauey of the International Crane Foundation (ICF) in Baraboo, Wisconsin, and born like the wild Whoopers in Canada, made his companion "Tex" along with Allen's "Josephine" one of the most famous tall white birds of all time. Archibald's story is an important one, and you will hear much more of him later.

White Crane Josephine

Like Allen's photo of the five migrant Whooping Cranes in Nebraska, it took far more labor-intensive and hazardous work, coupled with a great deal of luck for him to obtain a pair of potential breeding Cranes and to study the Whoopers with his ever-minute care.

The story of pairing "Josephine," resident in the New Orleans Zoo with "Old Devil" also in captivity at the Gothenburg Gun Club in Nebraska is an incredible one. For these two survivors of "shot and shell," each wounded in some way, were the only two captive Whoopers available in all of the world.

The story couples extravagant good luck with dire misfortune — alternating hope and despair — in that paradoxical way experiences come into our own lives and the lives of those — human and animal — we grow to care about. For any naturalist who is deeply occupied in that grand and capricious realm of nature — starting at the primal hunters, then to farmers and to shepherds to today's biologists and to any bird watcher with a spotting scope — there is always an intense element, sometimes joyous sometimes bitterly disappointing, of surprise.

According to legend, Ibycus (550 B.C.) was murdered at sea, and his murderers were discovered through cranes that followed the ship. Hence, the "cranes of Ibycus" became a proverb for the agency of the gods in revealing crime.

as used in
ZENOBIUS
Proverbs

Pied-De-Grue: Josephine

A Louisiana "White Lake Survivor," the Whooping Crane's esteemed chronicler Faith McNulty says of Josephine's pedigree. And survivor Josephine was, for she was a Louisiana Crane, "une grue blanche," a white Crane of the Old South.

With a life of extreme peril, Josephine's survival was in many ways as dramatic as Scarlett O'Hara's of *Gone with the Wind* fame. Josephine's life and with it her precious genetic material, could have certainly "gone with the wind" in 1940. Certainly, the peril to life and wing was comparable to Miss Scarlett's literary and symbolic loss in the South of the Civil War. For the white Crane was one of the few survivors of a powerful hurricane. A wind estimated at around one hundred miles per hour was followed by torrential rains which devastated the Louisiana Whooping Cranes and their territory near White Lake, a marshy area at the very southwestern edge of the Louisiana shore of the Gulf Coast.

Just after the time Richard Kleberg counted the Whooping Cranes on the King Ranch, Cranes which seemed to comprise a separate flock from the Aransas area regulars, a third group of white Cranes, was discovered in Louisiana by John Lynch, US Fish and Wildlife biologist. "Responding to a report of nesting activity in May 1939," Lynch discovered by aerial survey that thirteen adult Whooping Cranes and two "young of the year" comprised a resident — therefore, a non-migratory group (unlike the Aransas Cranes) near White Lake, and perhaps reproductively isolated from the migrating Cranes of Texas.

But the hurricane in the late summer of 1940 dispersed the Louisiana Cranes and reduced the population of thirteen Cranes to six in all. The six Cranes returned to the White Lake marshlands after the storm abated. Those storm survivors remained there, but their number dwindled over the years until only one Crane was left in 1947.

Of the other seven, six of them were "presumed shot, and the seventh, though wounded by gunshot survived" (McNulty). This surviving Crane "with a crippled wing" was captured from a rice field. It was taken to the Audubon Park Zoo (no relation to the Audubon Society) in New Orleans for safe keeping. A true survivor of storm and shot, this new zoo resident was Josephine.

Within her tall white body spiraled the only hope biologists had of preserving the genetic material of the Louisiana Cranes.

The remaining White Lake group, no doubt weakened by storm and flood continued to decline each year "until 1945," according to Gay M. Gomez of the University of Texas, "two birds remained" and five years later the last solitary wild hold-out "was chased by Allen and Lynch" and captured.

Aboard the helicopter with the Crane no doubt in summer molt, Lynch and Allen dubbed her/him "Mac" in honor of their pilot who had dropped them off in the swamp to capture the Crane. Allen was permitted to take Mac to Aransas to be released back into the wild. But Mac, an intruder on the migrant Whoopers' territory, did not survive. That left only Josephine.

Allen went to see Josephine, a growing Audubon Park Zoo attraction in New Orleans. But even though she was a "rare bird" indeed, when Allen went there to observe her captive behavior, he noted ironically that s/he was not quite the big attraction as the "Nile Hippos."

The problem of determining gender was still with Allen, and he pondered the question as to whether "this bird is male or female is impossible to decide" (McNulty). But Allen, as he notes in *Vanishing*, always covered the gender mystery by giving the birds "bisexual names." Josephine's name could be trans-sexed to "Jo." "Old Devil," the only other Whooping Crane, had a name change to "Petunia" which could be converted to "Pete."

The crane is a sacred bird. Its cries are most clear. They are heard at a distance of more than eight miles. I kept two cranes in a bamboo grove surrounding my lute hall. Sometimes in a shadow place they would dance together, other times they would fly upward and cry in unison. . . . They did not dance unless there was a cool breeze to shake their feathers, and they did not cry unless they could look up at the Milky Way as if they saw the gods.

CHINESE LUTE COMPOSER
Ming Dynasty

Vive La Difference

Because both Crane sexes look alike, with feathers colored the same, biologists in the field, even today, may find it tricky to determine a Crane's gender. It was not until 1962 that a biologist, Roxy Laybourne, "developed a new instrument for examining a bird's sexual organs while the bird is still alive. Previously, a bird's sex could only be confirmed during a necropsy or by observing a pair for conclusive behavioral data" (Katz). The less invasive method of observing sexual distinctions by posture and call was not around in Allen's time. The Canadian-born scientist George Archibald who hit upon this method was yet unborn. And, of course, the use of determining sex through DNA of the feather was far in the future.

Pygmy at war with a Crane— fragment of a terra-cotta altar, Corinth, *6th century B.C.*

But even today approaching a "warlike" Crane can still be tricky. A formidable task. However, Stephen Nesbitt, active in the Florida restoration of Whooping Cranes (mentioned earlier — and more of it will be discussed later), worked together with two other scientists, Clinton T. Moore and Kathleen Williams of the Florida Game and Fresh Water Fish Commission, and tackled the problem of the Sandhill gender in field work and presented their conclusions in a paper given to the Sixth Annual Crane Workshop in 1991.

In their opening paragraph, Nesbitt and colleagues speak of Cranes "in hand." It is important to remember that "in hand" is the scientist's very neutral shorthand for a perilous situation when it comes to Cranes — Sandhills or the larger and more ferocious Whooper. For these great birds, the Cranes, "do not go gently" into the hand — which may be an important step in sexing a bird — Sparrow or Crane.

There are stories of Crane hazards running through literature. "Many men," writes A.C. Bent, "have been injured by the Whooping Crane's savage thrusts." Bent goes on to quote Allen's hero Ernest Thompson Seton who reports an "extraordinary tragedy" happening in Canada in 1879. A young man, an Indian, possibly Cree, went hunting for wildfowl. "A white crane flew low within range and fell to the shot of the gun. As it lay on the ground, wounded in both wing and leg, crippled and helpless, [the young hunter] reached forward to seize it. But it drove its bill with all its force into his eye. The brain was pierced and the young hunter fell on the body of his victim."

Bent had many more stories to tell in his "Life History" of the Cranes but if you feel they come from a far distant past, I assure you I have seen with my own eyes what Cranes can do with that sharp bill of theirs — not to mention their claws.

In Nebraska, there primarily to watch the Sandhills mass, I took a side trip up to the farm of a noted aviculturist who was most hospitable. He showed me around his neat pens, some rare game birds and then my particular favorites the Whooper Swans. Finally, he strolled over to the Sandhill's enclosure. Inside the ample enclosure I saw two Florida Sandhills — the subspecies Nesbitt writes about. This aviculturist was engaged in an effort to help save the injured Florida Sandhills. He opened the gate in a gentlemanly fashion to give me room to put my long range camera lens through the opening. I happened to look down at his arms bare to the elbow and they were deeply scarred.

"Cranes?" I asked.

He nodded yes.

Thus, Cranes in the hand may be hazardous to an aviculturist's or biologist's eyes, ears, and hands. Consequently, though they didn't acknowledge the peril, probably because their audience is composed of seasoned biologists, Nesbitt and his colleagues hit upon a way to sex Florida Sandhills by measurement.

But before the three scientists could carry out the weighing and measuring process, they had to separate the Sandhills into their subspecies categories. Size is important and also range and distribution of the subspecies of Sandhills — for there are six categories or subspecies of *Grus canadensis* — and only one species of Whooper *(Grus americana)*.

The Florida scientists could eliminate some Sandhill subspecies by the mere fact that those subspecies are not found wild in Florida. Therefore, the Lesser Sandhill Crane *(Grus canadensis canadensis)*, the most northern flyer of all, did not have to be considered. This is the Sandhill which may go on to Siberia and winter in California, New Mexico, and North Texas. In addition, the Canadian Sandhill *(Grus canadensis rowani)* which

Sandhill Crane feet have very sharp claws. When a Crane is threatened, it will use it's wings to maintain balance and then jump up and strike at the attacker with it's feet.

109

intergrade with the Lesser has about the same range as the Lesser but doesn't appear to go much farther north or west than Canada's British Columbia.

Eliminating those two subspecies leaves two other Sandhill subspecies living in what are called "disjunct populations." In other words, these Cranes stay put in their locale and their flock is cut-off from other Sandhill subspecies. They are the Mississippi Sandhill *(Grus canadensis pulla)*. Its slender flock is so small that it is considered endangered. It resides in one single county, Jackson County, Mississippi both winter and summer.

Finally, the Florida scientists could also eliminate the Cuban Sandhill *(Grus canadensis nesiotes)* residents of Cuba and about which much has lately been discovered through an ICF study in Castro's island.

What Nesbitt, Moore, and Williams have left to study in Florida are of course the resident Florida Sandhills *(Grus canadensis pratensis)* that is also a disjunct population and does not migrate. Also they have the Greater Sandhills *(Grus canadensis tabida)*, the holotype of Sandhills given the classification by Linnaeus in 1758. This Greater may be seen wintering here in Texas and also migrating to winter in Florida (Johnsgard).

Therefore, with Florida stay-at-homes and winter migrant Greaters, the three scientists color-marked them by seasonal separation to denote Florida Sandhill (FSH) and Greater Sandhill (GSH). By disallowing those Cranes which they dubbed TCTC (too-close-to-call), they came up with the measurements that showed first of all in either gender of GSH: they were heavier, shorter legged, and longer billed than FSH. But bills were longer on males of either sub-species. The difference in bill length was greater in GSH than FSH.

If you are crouched in a blind beside the Platte River in those overwhelming moments at twilight watching five hundred thousand Sandhills flying through skies to roost mid-river, or you're touring the desert beauties of Bosque del Apache New Mexico and photographing hundreds of Sandhills or one or two Whoopers at dawn, or you're tracking the Florida population as Nesbitt and colleagues did, the "Gender Prediction from Measurements" by Nesbitt, Moore, and Williams might seem so much scientific minutia. However it is important to remember that these sometimes small increments of scientific knowledge are the way of "doing" science, building layer upon layer.

Fifty years ago, Allen had no such statistical and empirical data concerning the Whooping Crane. He did have many facts concerning the

Sandhills available to him through the work of Dr. Lawrence Walkinshaw, a Michigan dentist.

Dr. Walkinshaw's first sight of Cranes so galvanized him that he was drawn over the margins of his daily routine into the Crane realm. It was a Michigan sight near his home, he writes, "which completely changed my life." And he describes this experience:

Tapestry depicting a Crane as one of the birds of the Fifth Day of Creation, Spanish, *11th century*. *(Museu de la Catedral, Girona)*

"Roaming over a ridge from which groves of old beech had recently been lumbered, I heard a loud call vibrating from the marsh ahead, reverberating between the bordering wood. What made this wild haunting call? Wading forward through the muck and water at the ridge's base, pushing aside dense sedges and grass that hot afternoon, I saw ahead of me three tremendous birds, almost four feet tall watching intently." *(Cranes of the World)*

From that moment on in 1930, after seeing the Sandhill Cranes, Walkinshaw became one of the most intense Crane watchers of the world. No place was too far or too inaccessible for him. Up and down the flyways he traveled. In the U.S. and abroad, as well, he went in search of Cranes, even to the extent of helping with the search for the Whooper's nesting grounds.

Once, he literally wore out a pair of shoes in search of Crowned Cranes in Africa. He found them, a nesting pair with three not the usual two eggs, and, although his credentials in one branch of life science, dentistry, made him certifiably a professional, in avian research he was technically an amateur. An "amateur," however, in the true sense of the word's origins: as one enormously devoted to an endeavor. And he was distinctly professional in his manner of compiling data on the Sandhills for his book *The Sandhill Cranes* published in 1949 and later *Cranes of the World.*

Robert Porter Allen had Walkinshaw's work to aid him in his Aransas Crane study, and he sometimes had Walkinshaw in person beside him in the field. At one time Walkinshaw watched Josephine devour a count of "800 grasshoppers," and carefully noted this fact in his precise records.

Pete: The Old Devil in Disguise

No doubt after much paperwork and Crane diplomacy, Allen successfully negotiated the arrival at Aransas of Josephine, from her eight years as a zoo resident in New Orleans, and Old Devil from his long tenure in Nebraska. These were the only captive Whooping Cranes in the world. Whether or not they were male or female was a matter of chance. Allen took that chance.

"Old Devil" also a survivor was rescued from a Nebraska field by farmers. He was wounded in a wing and in an eye, and the farmer took what he thought to be an enormous white Heron to the Gothenburg Gun Club for sanctuary. "Some Heron" Allen remarked in 1936. From that year, "Old Devil" languished at the sanctuary in lonely and un-paired splendor, never compromising his lofty and well-placed mistrust of human beings. Living a life of "silence, exile and cunning" for twelve years until he was trucked down from Nebraska in 1948.

The Nebraska Whooper, although technically still captive, was placed in an Aransas enclosure, a one hundred fifty acre tract of brackish marsh, so large that it had to be a kind of heady freedom for "Old Devil" now dubbed "Petunia" (to be on the safe side as mentioned earlier). The name was ultimately trans-sexed to "Pete" when s/he did indeed turn out to be a male.

It wasn't long that spring until Allen and his colleagues of the USFWS team beheld the field with soaring hopes. Neither of the pair was young, but the two Cranes danced and paired like newlyweds. Finally Josephine laid two eggs in her great ground nest "of salt-flatgrass, cattail and sea oxeye" with Allen making sometimes minute-by-minute log entries.

But even though the two large speckled ovate Whooping Crane eggs were hatched, the first Whooper eggs ever produced in captivity, they proved, alas, to be infertile. The hopes of Allen and the team along with the watchers of the world were dashed; the Cranes themselves, with that canny Crane wisdom, smashed the eggs. Shortly after that Allen found Pete dead, "simply toppled over of causes," gallant and crusty to the end of his long life.

Josephine, lone survivor of hurricane and hunter, was again a survivor — this time a widow.

Recovering from the setback, Allen looked around and realized there was another eligible Crane. One called "Crip," by then a year-round resident of Aransas, wounded like his predecessor Pete and unable to migrate. Crip was hustled from the field and placed with Josephine.

Amazingly she accepted him. Not always a sure thing with these aristocratic and (mostly) monogamous birds. As Allen put it, "They became more than friends."

The pulse of the Aransas team surely started to race when Crip and Josephine paired, performed their astonishing bonding ritual of dance and began nesting. Allen watched the two Cranes from an observation tower as they became the solicitous guardians of their single precious egg. Of course, the egg was not only special to the future Crane parents, but in the egg nestled the hope of the world for the preservation of this species, this most rare of all the world's Cranes. The wild population that year of 1950 stood at thirty-four. From the time the count began in 1938 it, too, was a "record high." And the single egg of Josephine and Pete had the potential to add one more Crane to the count and one more chance to preserve the life form of its scarce genetic inheritance.

Woodcut by
PIERIO VELERIANOS, *1604.*

By night, the crane
a pebble gripped
doth hold
Lest sleep surprise
his watch and
close his eyes
So lest this world
should lull
with pomp & gold
The Cross reminds us
where our duty lies

EMBLEM BOOK OF
HOHBERG, *1675*

Portrait of Rusty as a Young Crane

In late May of 1950, Allen and the USFWS team would listen to hear the high piping note of a just-hatched Crane. A sound no human had heard for almost thirty years.

"Rusty" the downy young Whooping Crane chick entered the world shielded by his conspicuously white guardian parents and protected by his natural brownish orange color, a characteristic of all the Crane's family (with of course a few exceptions). Allen knew the tiny Crane had pipped only because the "behavior of the parent birds" made it seem certain that the hoped for "miracle had taken place" *(Vanishing)*.

An anxious night passed. Then, next day Allen saw him: "so tiny I could barely believe my eyes, but there was a rusty downy thing moving about on the nest on wobbly legs." The first Whooping Crane ever hatched in captivity had stepped out of its spaceship egg and arrived safely on terra firma!

From a distance, Allen watched the parents care for their mottled reddish brown chick. When Rusty ran "between the towering columns of Crip's legs ... Crip bent over, and with a soft and graceful tenderness, and finding the tiny mouth with the tip of his great bill, fed him. In all my experience with birds, this was the most wonderful" *(Vanishing)*.

A crane chick in normal hatching position.
Drawing by Kate Spencer

Rusty lived four days, four days in which Allen logged every movement, every gesture of parents and young, absorbing and recording in that short space of time as much knowledge of Crane behavioral lore as he possibly could. Meanwhile the parents stood guard, never leaving the young chick.

On the final day, Allen sensed by the parents' behavior that something had gone wrong. The heretofore extremely cautious parent Cranes had left the nesting area, and appeared casually feeding at a distance. Allen and the team entered the always Crane-guarded enclosure with the usually wary at-attention parents "scarcely seeming to notice." "Rusty had vanished." The only sign of life around the abandoned nest was the distinct mark of Raccoon tracks *(Vanishing)*.

Two years later when Allen published his land-mark *Whooping Crane Research Report* the wild population returning to Aransas dropped again. This time it fell to twenty-two, down significantly from the "record high" of thirty-four the year Rusty hatched. Allen and the USFWS team knew that the only hope lay in the wild population. For, compounding the ill-fated loss of Rusty, the New Orleans Zoo demanded Josephine's return from Aransas. And because officialdom decided

Newly-born Cranes are "precocial" birds—hatched with feathers, can see and hear, and leave the nest with parents in two days.

— with some wisdom behind the decision — against breaking up a mated pair, Crip left his semi-wild existence at Aransas to live with Josephine in the Zoo in New Orleans.

After a long unproductive spell, the two Cranes, the first to do so in captivity, would produce eggs season after season — a total of fifty-two. Some of the eggs were infertile, some viable, but more than one was inadvertently destroyed — by the Cranes or through human error. Despite this situation, four hatchling Cranes would survive to maturity, the first ever.

However, like the hurricane which took Josephine's Louisiana flock, ultimately leaving her the lone survivor, a storm shaped from human nature would rage over the Crane's survival. The storm would swirl across North America in exchanges and verbal forays. These tempestuous times of the '50s and '60s have been amply chronicled by Faith McNulty and Jerome J. Pratt.

The Secretary of the Interior Stuart Udall wrote the "Introduction" to Faith McNulty's *The Whooping Crane* in which he summed up the story as one of "devotion and dedication to a bird," citing Allen particularly, and then noting that there were "Human miscalculations, greed, neglect, skill," as well as "monumental efforts of agencies both private and government to locate the nesting grounds." But in those days, everything done for the captive Cranes and the wild ones captured was entirely new territory. Exploring McNulty's chronicle as well as Robin Doughty's and Jerome Pratt's, I now realize even more what a slender hold the Whooping Crane had on this planet, and the desperate awakening consciousness of those who formed, in McNulty's words, an "ever-widening circle" of interest in the great white Cranes.

But in retrospect, the many perspectives on the Crane's welfare within this ornithological tempest shared a common cause, the Crane's survival. Somehow or other the distinguished Crane ombudsmen appear to be like members of an extended family, grandparents, in-laws, parents, and siblings, their unity asunder, while meanwhile the center of their concern (in this case the Whooper) goes about the business of enduring. Remembering how new the business of breeding these great birds in captivity was, I think about the wisdom of poet Robert Haas's lines "All the new thinking is about loss/ In this, it resembles old thinking."

But as it happens with discouraging loss, Nature may take over and a new pathway may be found. Good news from the north would come in time. Consequently time and nature would indicate that those who were speaking out firmly for wildness as well as those who professed to saving the species by rearing them in captivity could find a common territory upon which to meet — or at least to adapt.

Back in the car parked near the observation tower, I start up and drive slowly, finishing the loop open to Aransas visitors. Just past the Visitor Center, where the "1000-hour volunteer" is certainly logging more hours toward her second millennium of volunteerism, I stop for one last photograph. As I step to the side of the road, an Armadillo, its brown armor blazing in the sun like the Spanish blue of a Conquistador's armor, scuttles through the long brown grass. And suddenly in the shadow of the motte of Live Oaks directly in front of me, like moving shadows of the trees themselves, six Sandhill Cranes proceed in single file, a dignified procession barely visible.

The clump of trees the gray-brown Cranes walk beneath shields a view of marshy Heron Flats and the reach of the Gulf beyond. The white Crane pair is no doubt searching the shallows for Blue Crabs unconcerned as they were three hours ago when I photographed them on the lower contour of ground.

Adolescent Whooper.

Allen noted this distinction in the behavioral preferences of the two species, the Sandhills staying above the shoreline and the Whoopers feeding in the marshlands. The sight of the Sandhills is a kind of verification of his accurate eye.

The destiny of the Whooping Crane, recorded migrating so often during its more plentiful past of a century ago, flying in twos or threes like white and shining marks among their more plentiful gray-brown cousins would intersect with Sandhills in the twentieth century biological field experiment. It would be, starting in 1975, a more than a decade long experiment that would demand enormous energy, with biologists covering great distances near the Arctic in Canada to Grays Lake in the Yellowstone area. And the Sandhills would become "foster parents" to the Whoopers.

Japanese swordguard, made of iron, showing a stylized Crane, *17th century*.

Bent on saving the Whooping Crane, biologists of the experimental program would explore some new methods of captive breeding in the wild. Some of the answers would be "No." And nature would follow a new pathway. But just as Allen found when the way seemed blocked after Rusty's death, and the Crane parents returned to a zoo, not all is lost. With patient learning, scientists up to now, after much trial and error, find some results which open onto new concepts about this most studied and endangered bird, the Whooping Crane, arguably one of the most documented and publicized avian creatures in the world.

I leave the Refuge, sighting again the great spiral smoke of a controlled burn-off in the distance. Then I make the turn near Austwell. Heading south to Corpus Christi, the fifty-year-old dream of the wild population started in Robert Porter Allen's and his colleagues' minds follows me. In Corpus, I will board a plane and fly northward, just as the white Cranes will do in a few months. However, they will go on to Canada, landing in their summer nesting grounds, a place mysterious and unknown to the biologists of Allen's day as the entire North American continent was to the sixteenth century explorers who prowled its coasts in their mysterious sailing vessels the Carancahua must have looked upon as white winged birds.

Aboard the plane flying north, I look down from a Crane's eye view as we make the take-off turn, the plane's silver wing flexing like a living tissue. Below the wing is the white sparkle of Corpus Christi, the city's rooftops looking like so many microchips on a computer motherboard. Beyond that, the wide loose French curve of the shore, shielded by barrier islands, an oil tanker clearly visible, cuts its way through the channel in the protection of the Intra-Coastal Waterway, its wake eternally washing away shoreline.

I think how almost a century and a half ago, the Carancahua paddled off from Matagorda Island into extinction. And that, in 1682, the great explorer Sieur, Cavalier de La Salle returned to the New World from France and sailed off-course right up to the harbor, certain that he had returned to the exact spot he had found two years previously — the mouth of the Mississippi. Not realizing his error, off-course hundreds of nautical miles, he stepped forth onto the beach of Matagorda and planted the French flag firmly in the sand, announcing the claim of the King. Thus, the great explorer unwittingly unfurled one of Texas's six famous flags over the land of the great Lone Star state which was also claimed for the Spanish king more than one hundred years before.

Just a little farther north, the sprawl of green and water-pocked acreage of Aransas National Wildlife Refuge stretches to the east of us. Its amorphous shape of natural habitat, contrasts with the grid of roads, houses, and farms, the last *oikos*, the chosen winter household of Whooping Cranes in this precious ecozone.

Discoveries of the
Noblest Flyers

*Suddenly, across one of those glimpses of
eternity, there flocked the forms of two majestic birds;
and from them came a far croaking trumpet sound.
By their long wings, long necks, long legs and snowy
plumes, I later knew they were two white cranes,
the noblest thing that flies, sailing on to their
northern home, and the ring triumphant of that
stirring trumpet call still echoes in my heart.*

ERNEST THOMPSON SETON
Trail of the Artist-Naturalist, 1940

Crane Histories: Ancient and Modern

Carlos, a tall lanky teacher and scholarly historian ascends the steps of the Episcopal Church pulpit. There to commemorate the life of one of his former prep school students who died of AIDS before the age of thirty, Carlos holds up a paper Crane, one folded in the Japanese origami style.

Although he has the kind of voice strong enough to fill a classroom or a church, he does not say a word. He strikes a match, and, with magisterial demeanor, holds it beneath the paper Crane. It bursts into flame illuminating the faces of those assembled, the young man's parents and friends. The fire consumes the folded image to ash, but deftly, Carlos replaces the ash with another paper Crane. He has made his point.

As a knowledgeable historian, Carlos draws upon the deepest levels of the ancient: the Crane as an image of hope, of transformation, and of renewal. It is a symbol which delves like a Crane's bill into the earthen layers of ancient times and ancient cultures.

In this particular instance, and with historical keenness, Carlos has opened a magnificent catalogue of stories, both ancient and modern, and, without a word, he has with one image compounded several cultural beliefs.

With the Japanese culture, it is the stirring concept of a "thousand Cranes" folded in honor of another lost young life, the child Sadako, who, dying of radiation burns, tried to fold a thousand Cranes. Sadako is still honored by school children around the world by folding the origami thousand Cranes in her honor. It is a story told earlier in these pages, but one that bears repeating, for it too is a modern story drawing upon ancient Japanese belief and religion.

In Shinto Japan, one story is of a simple fisherman who leaves home to wed the daughter of the Dragon King and to live with her in the King's palace under the sea. Longing for home, the fisherman returns to his land only to find that he is an old, old man, away over two hundred years. Distraught, he opens a little cask his princess wife gave him. He is transformed into a

The Red-Crowned Crane has long been revered throughout China and Japan as a symbol of fidelity in marriage, of good luck, of long life, and of love. Adapted to colder weather by their large body size, their breeding grounds are in the Amur River basin near the China-Russia border. A substantial population live year-around on Japan's Hokkaido Island.

Tale of the Tsuru

Once, long ago, a mighty warrior hunting with his falcon felled a magnificent tsuru (Japanese crane). The crane, driven to the feet of the warrior, did not cower but instead looked the man straight in the face, prepared to die with dignity and honor. The warrior, overcome with admiration for its spirit and courage, released the noble bird. Vowing never to hunt again, he retired to a Buddhist monastery where he became a poet and lived to a very great age. And from that time to this, the tsuru has symbolized long life, courage and good fortune.

long-lived Crane, and she appears to him as a Turtle. They live on happily together Crane and Turtle for at least a thousand years *(Mythology of All Races)*.

This story of transformation later became a part of Buddhist tradition, and, in the year 1611 according to Britton and Hayashida, "the theme of *senbazuru* or 'thousand cranes' was executed on a fifteen-meter scroll of that title" in which appeared the "myriad images of Cranes by the artist Sotatsu" combined with the calligraphy of poems by "thirty-six classical Japanese poets" (Britton and Hayashida).

When Carlos set the origami Crane aflame and allowed it to kindle to ashes only to be replaced by a freshly folded Crane's image, he was drawing upon his own culture's familiar story of the Phoenix. One that begins in ancient Egyptian times and endures through works of classical Greek and Roman authors and into the Judeo-Christian culture, appearing in one Old Testament version in the words of that great Biblical sufferer Job, who said, "I shall die in my nest, and I shall multiply like the Phoenix."

With origins in the distant past of ancient Egypt, the story of the Phoenix may be traced to the works of the Greek "father of history" Herodotus in the Fifth Century B.C. "Fascinated" by exploration, Herodotus set off on a journey around the rim of the known world, the civilizations clustered around the shores of the Mediterranean *(Birth of Western Civilization)*.

Crossing and recrossing the sea which he knew from Homer's *Odyssey*, a poetic history composed three centuries before, Herodotus realized he could find himself on waters so perilous that, in Homer's words: "not even the Cranes with their great strength will cross it." But after surviving many journeys, Herodotus returned to write his travels and his history. He wrote, not in poetry as his historical predecessor Homer, but in prose. Among the many wonders he reported, his stay in Egypt, a civilization at least four thousand years older than his own Greek civilization's time, impressed him greatly.

He noted the Egyptians' veneration of animals, of cats or of birds, their Ibis, particularly sacred to them, "with legs like a Crane's." Among the many natural curiosities he solved was the mystery of the Crane's disappearance from Europe each winter on migration. He writes: "The cranes, when they flee from the rigors of northern winters, flock to Egypt to pass the cold season."

A century later, the great naturalist and philosopher Aristotle reinforced this migratory knowledge of the Greeks, saying that "these birds migrate from the steppes [of Russia] to the marshland south of Egypt where the Nile has its source."

But one mystery was not solved: the location of the nesting area. Later, in the seventeenth century, the Reverend Edward Topsell comments that because "the cranes breed so far from the sight and conversation of men, none of the Ancients [Greeks/Romans] did ever make mention of their sitting or hatching their young" (*Fowls of Heaven*).

The Egyptians' long familiarity with Cranes is clearly evident in their art. Their civilization dated by their astronomers back to what they called "First Time," has a long history of depicting Cranes on their temple reliefs. As far back as several thousand years before Herodotus's appearance in Egypt, species of Cranes are portrayed quite accurately and are easily recognizable. Take, for example, the temple relief of Queen Hatshepsut's Tomb, Eighth Dynasty, depicting three figures marching in a procession. Two of the figures, one in front, one in back, are human bearers, their heads in profile, their torsos and limbs depicted in the tradition of Egyptian art with their feet turned sideways. But the center figure of the three is a Demoiselle Crane,

More than 4000 years ago, a child playing with his pet crane and baboon was depicted on the wall of an Offering Chapel for Nefermaat at Meidum, Egypt

125

portrayed as in nature, and calmly walking with the humans as if it were a part of the group, and going to its fate, no doubt, as accompaniment to the Queen's afterlife.

Another relief of the Old Kingdom, Fifth Dynasty, shows again two human attendants, but this time they are herding an entire "troop" of Cranes, Eurasian and Demoiselle intermixed. This relief is shown in a photograph by Carl Von Treuenfels, German President of the World Wild Life Fund who not only photographed Crane artworks worldwide from the Orient to Africa but also depicted the fifteen species of Cranes including the Whooper and Sandhill. His work *Kraniche: Vogel des Glucks* (*Cranes: Birds of Good Luck*) is a landmark of historical and naturalistic Crane research. Published in 1998, the "Good Luck" in the title of *Kraniche* pays tribute to the long cultural notion of the Crane as a bird of good fortune and long life.

Besides the natural history reports of Cranes as well as other birds and animals venerated by the Egyptians, Herodotus tells of seeing a bird "pictured" but a bird he never actually saw in feather or flesh. The Egyptians, says Herodotus, call this strange creature the Bennu bird, and Herodotus, in relating its story, comments that he had some reservations about it.

However, it seems that this strange bird, the Bennu, after a long period flies into the sacred city of the sun, Heliopolis (now buried beneath modern Cairo). There the bird alights and builds its nest.

Because the bird is sacred to the sun-god Ra, the sun kindles the nest into a fire consuming the bird and nest to ash. This occasion marks the end of a long era. But a renewal of time occurs: a new bird transformed from the ash arises. Herodotus calls the Bennu bird in his language the "phoinix." He says, though again he admits he has never actually seen it, he believes the phoenix to be "like an eagle." Later sources and some paintings depict the Bennu as a great waterbird: Crane or Heron.

Down through the centuries, Roman historians, using Herodotus as a source, amplify the story, and rather than the five hundred year period Herodotus established as the end of one time and the beginning of another time, Pliny, The Elder in the First Century A.D. in his *Natural Histories* states that the bird's metamorphosis is the occasion of the Sothic eon, a period of some one thousand four hundred sixty years.

Consequently, the Romans of Pliny's time, wishing to honor their new emperor, Caesar Antonius, the Pius, caused a four drachma coin to

Drawing of coin (drachma) struck in honor of Caesar Antonius showing a haloed Crane.

be struck in the city of Alexandria in the year 139 A.D. On the coin is a "nimbate" Crane. Its head encircled by a halo, it is a recognizable image of a Wattled Crane depicted as a Phoenix. Also impressed on the coin is the Greek word "Aion," from which we derive "eon." The coin bearing the Crane's image is a clear symbol of renewal. And indeed, it was. For Antonius's reign, beginning the year before the coin's date, was a kind of Golden Age followed by terror. And the hope for an afterlife was inspired not by the Caesars but by the professions of a simple man from the east, put to death by crucifixion. The Romans considered as a "cult," the Christians, followers of Christ. Later Christians absorbed the symbol of the Phoenix as one of Resurrection.

Although it has been a religious symbol, the symbol of the Phoenix is also evident it the secular world of today. It appears on the U.S. map with Phoenix, Arizona, built on the ruins of an earlier civilization, the Hohokam, and farther west in Mountain View, California on a star map with "Project Phoenix," a scientific endeavor of the Institute of the Search for Extraterrestrial Intelligence — SETI. Project Phoenix, says Jeff Greenwald, is focused on observing "one thousand sunlike stars all within two hundred light years of earth, collecting radio signals over a vast range of frequencies" (*Discover*).

Hohokam pottery design,
Southern Arizona,
12th century A.D.

Heliopolis to Helicopter

The two governments of the United States and Canada, governments established in countries far beyond the rim of the known world of Herodotus's time or even Caesar Antonius's day, did not issue special coins to mark the "new era" of the Whooping Crane in 1954. However, they did issue stamps. Canada was first, with a handsome blue and white line drawing of a Whooper pair flying above a wetland, issued the spring following the discovery. Two years later, the U.S. issued a stamp with the Whooping Crane's image painted by noted wildlife artist Bob Hines for a conservation series of four animals. The Whooping Crane was the second wild bird, other than the national Eagle, to be pictured as "a central theme" on a U.S. stamp. It was preceded by the Wild Turkey (*Birds in Our Lives*).

Canadian stamp issued in honor of the discovery of Whooping Crane nesting area.

After years of fruitless searching by Allen and the Audubon Society, the U.S. Fish and Wildlife Service and the Canadian Wildlife Service, the discovery of the nesting area was found by accident — no doubt the way many discoveries have been in the past and will be made in the future.

The story has all the elements of Herodotus's tale of the Bennu bird for it involves like the story of the Phoenix: fire and ash — and a renewed hope. Even today, fifty years later, the place in which the Crane's breeding area was found in some ways looks as if it is yet beyond the world's rim. And, in the Reverend Topsell's words still "far from the sight and conversation of [most]."

Look at a modern map of Canada, and you will see an almost inconceivably blank area stretching its many icy fingers into the Arctic Sea above the orderly shapes of the lower Provinces, their southern baselines delineated by the U.S./Canada border. This area, the Northwest Territories, with few roads and few railroads, to this day must be traveled mostly by plane. So large, the Territories have been split in half with the eastern portion called "Nunavik." Modern Canadian tour books generally include an entry about the Territories saying something of them such as

"Few Canadians living in the Provinces have ever visited this area, and most know little of it."

The final days of June in 1954, a Canadian Forest Service helicopter took off in response to a forest fire, kindled possibly naturally in the immense reaches of Wood Buffalo National Park Refuge, a refuge established in 1927 to save the Wood Bison. Most sources do not give the cause of the fire, but the Forest Service pilot and his passenger upon returning homeward from their investigation looked down into the Ice Age remnants of ponds, swamps and Black Spruce to see a most miraculous sight. Near the area of the Sass River they beheld "a tall and gleaming white Whooping Crane pair," and with them, "a long legged rusty little bird — the size of a rooster — a Whooping Crane chick" (McNulty).

Fast as sparks from dry timber, the news flew across the Crane Conservationist world spreading like an uncontrolled forest fire. At last the few tempting reports of sighting Cranes in this vast area which surfaced in 1953 were actually verified and the location pinpointed on the map in the summer of 1954. The discovery was as important to the hopeful of the Crane world as the discovery of a mother lode of copper had been to Samuel Hearne, one of the earliest of European and most intrepid of explorers of the Northwest Territories. Hearne, employed by the Hudson's Bay Company in 1773, was one of the first to make a valid report of the Whooping Crane in Canada. Yet, he was probably most known for his bold and long footsore walk across Canada where he discovered Great Slave Lake near Wood Buffalo.

United States stamp honoring the discovery.

In his report of his explorations, Hearne comments on the "Hooping Crane," saying that "this bird visits Hudson's Bay in the spring, though not in great numbers. They are generally seen only in pairs and that not very often .... The bird seldom has more than two young, and retires southward in the Fall."

Amazingly, with the exception of the Hudson's Bay location, the observations of the Whooping Crane are just about all the natural history of the Whooping Crane's wild breeding habits that were known over two hundred years later when the Canadian location of the breeding area was found in 1954.

Away from Aransas and in the Bahamas pursuing a summertime study of Flamingos, Robert Allen Porter was, of course, one of the first to hear the news via the Audubon Society. The following spring, as soon as the area was unlocked from its icy grip, Allen traveled to Wood Buffalo Wildlife Refuge. There, with a Canadian Wildlife Service biologist, he flew over the territory. From the air, they spotted a wild Whooping Crane on its nest, and, looking down, Allen notes, admiring its wildness that he could see the Crane "its yellow eye doubtless glaring at us with hostility and a total lack of fear."

While searching for Whooping Cranes in Canada, Allen must have thought of Ernest Thompson Seton. Seton, whose stories of the Canadian woods inspired Allen to characterize his own youth as that of a "Seton Indian," found inspiration in the prairie and woodland of Canada.

Once, when young, Seton sighted Whooping Cranes, "the noblest flyers. "And, in his old age, he writes: "What would I not give to hear them, and see them with those same young eyes ... that glorious bird is gone — forever."

Like his hero, Allen too would slog it out on the ground, trekking across near impassable Canadian terrain, exploring places impossible even for a helicopter to land. A vast country which had so few landmarks that with a slight navigational error, Allen's helicopter pilot put him down in the wrong place — distant from the nesting Cranes. Allen and his companion were finally picked up from this venture, yet he made another try.

After again spending those many long, long northern days of summer in bog and swamp — "earthbound," he returned weary, unshaven, to be described by a newsman as looking like a "man from hell."

But he was happy. He had seen the Whoopers on the ground — but only once. The important thing, he writes, is: "the area is no longer unknown."

Terra Cognita: The Known Land

Now biologists could connect the final dots on the Whoopers' migratory flight path. Starting at the Gulf, and dashing up the center of the continent, they fly like white feathered divining rods above the deep buried watery recesses of the Ogallala Aquifer to stop at the Platte River on their spring journey to Canada.

After stoking up on the food-rich Platte and heading north for the final leg of their spring migration, the white Cranes veer more westerly. As if these birds could call up the Ice Age memory of their distant ancestors, they fly along the farthest western edge of what was once the Wisconsin Ice Age glacier. Still north and west they head up through the southern tip of Saskatchewan into Alberta, the province where the lower half of Wood Buffalo Wildlife Refuge lies. Finally they settle into their isolated nesting areas, at home in that watery zone of the Northwest Territories, in Canada — a territory only six thousand years ago, finally loosed from the hammerlock of glacial ice (*Landprints*).

German woodcut,
15th century.

Cranes teach us wisdom to weigh
our own selves, and what we want
in nature to supply by industry.
Wherefore when they fly they
carry a stone to give poise to
their bodies, and by the fall of that
stone as they fly aloft in the air
they can tell whether they are over
earth or water, when to rest and
when to go forward.

REV. EDWARD TOPSELL

From the People at the World's Rim

Cranes petroglyph,
Gulikson Glen, Wisconsin,
"probably Ojibwa"
(*circa 1750*), derived from
*Rock Art of the
American Indian.*

Like the Phoenix arising anew, the springtime arrival of Cranes in Canada announces summer's return. And their arrival is awaited by the Cree, Slavey, Chipewyan, and Assiniboin, the Amerindian Tribes who for centuries have ranged across this vast sub-arctic land. They look up to see Cranes in the sky at the season's turn.

Surviving the long winter, they tell stories of summer's renewal when the earth stirs with the richness of plant and animal. To such people who dwell in the far north, the change of season — the voyages of sun and moon across the sky — clearly establish the tenor of their lives.

On a clear moonlit night, say the Cree, an Algonquin tribe, you can see the Rabbit in the full of the moon. How Rabbit got his wish to go to the moon is one of the Cree's favorite children's stories.

It was Crane of all the birds, the only one to fly high enough and to have wings large enough that agreed to carry Rabbit to the moon. For Crane's good deed, Rabbit rewarded the great bird with a red crown.

Wearing its "red headdress" to this day, Crane flies neck and legs extended. Its legs, trailing like an earthbound afterthought, are so long because they are stretched by the burden of carrying Rabbit to the moon (*Flight*).

Because the winter is long and harsh, the signs of summer are clearly the occasion for joy and for some of their major ceremonies. But sometimes the people's stories have an element of pain as well, including the death of their favorite animals. And, because the Indian people have an accurate knowledge of the animals and the seasons, their tales frequently embody many natural truths.

The Assiniboin, the most northerly of the Great Plains tribes and a Siouan language group, tell how there was a time when there was no summer — only winter. The condition of prevailing winter is not without its element of geological truth. Most of Canada was once buried in thick ice, says geologist Walter Sullivan, and now "constitutes the world's largest area of glaciated terrain" (*Landprints*).

But the Assiniboin, living in a time of only winter, so the story goes, sent their hunters south following the migrating animals. One day the hunters came to a place where there is no snow. But the people who lived in the south, finding summer so precious, kept it in a bag guarded by warriors day and night.

The Assiniboin met in council and decided to send the fleetest animals south to bring summer to the people. Lynx, with the help of an Assiniboin hunter-guide, found the guarded place of summer and took the bag in its mouth. But as Lynx rushed away, it woke the southern warriors and they pursued it across the land.

Exhausted after a while, Lynx passed summer to Fox, and Fox to Antelope, and Antelope to Wolf. But when each animal passed summer to the other, the animal stopped, winded, and the southern warriors killed it. But Wolf kept running, and, as it sped northward, grass turned green and trees leafed out. Finally when Wolf crossed the frozen river, ice melted, halting the southern pursuers.

The Assiniboin decided to bargain with the southern tribes who also are of the Great Plains culture and celebrate summer each year with the Sun Dance. So the tribes agreed that each should keep summer for a time. And because the Cranes are the earliest to come north, the Assiniboin chose Crane to carry summer back and forth. Thus, because Cranes head south in a leisurely fashion during the fall months, the warm days leave the Assiniboin more slowly. However, because Cranes migrate northward more speedily in the spring, they will bring summer back to the people sooner (*Nihancan*).

Even though each story, the Cree's and Assiniboin's, takes a different form — Cree's a children's tale, the Assiniboin's more closely allied to a creation story — the common element of Cranes as a preference for carrying a burden is there. And this element may be found worldwide in myth and folktale.

In early China, it is said, Cranes bore the goddesses aloft, and later because the wise contemplative scholar is associated with soaring thoughts, the Cranes were chosen to bear the wise ones heavenward (*Flight*). In Europe, too, there has been a long tradition of believing migrating Cranes carry the little perching birds on their wings across the sea to Africa. Folklore? Human imagination gone awry? Perhaps. But an experienced wildlife guide has sworn to me that he has seen with his own eyes Hummingbirds nestle in the wings of Canada Geese for a free migratory ride northward.

Not only in folklore and story do Cranes know no human borders, but in nature they fly easily from one country to the next. The Siberian Crane (*Grus leucogeranus*), like the Whooper, a white feathered black wing-

Therefore the crane is associated with hsien-jeu, the Immortals: the crane is their favorite mount, and many a holy recluse is said to have disappeared from human sight riding on a crane.

The Lore of the Chinese Lute
(18th century story
of Hsien Huan)

"Snow Wreath," "Lily of Birds," "Crane with long black sleeves"are some of the names the Russians have for the Siberian Crane, *Grus leucogeranus*. The western and central flocks of Siberian Cranes migrate 3,700 miles from western Siberia to either India and Iran to winter, while the eastern flocks migrate 3,100 miles to central China from eastern Siberia.

tipped bird, flies the longest and farthest of any migratory Crane, well over five thousand miles. The mystery of its breeding range and migration routes has been as puzzling as the Whooper's. Perhaps because of the even more isolated areas of Siberia, Afghanistan, China, and other countries where it breeds or migrates, even more so. And the "Sibe," as ICF biologists call it, has engendered an internationally cooperative spirit among scientists of countries whose governments do not always see eye-to-eye, as, for example, the former Soviet Union and the U.S. during Cold War times.

Although the Siberian is more populous than the rarest Crane of all — the Whooper — it is also Endangered. To save it biologists have had to work together, skip across language barriers, pass through customs officials with their burden of precious eggs, and unsnarl government entanglements with the endurance — if not the ease — of a Crane flying across borders.

There has been much work toward this international cooperation spearheaded by the International Crane Foundation in Wisconsin since its founding a little over twenty-five years ago. But, arguably, the first truly international cooperative work with Cranes began with Canada and the U.S., traditionally friendly nations it is true, but each country, after all, does have a border and varying regulations. "The long-standing cooperation of the Canadian Wildlife Service and the U.S. Fish and Wildlife Services," writes Jerome J. Pratt, " in recovering the Whooping Crane from the virtual brink of extinction is a model of international cooperation for all nations."

One measure of the ease of cooperation between the two countries is that over three decades would pass with Canadian and U.S. biologists working together before the two governments would make their agreeable and cooperative spirit official in a "Memorandum of Understanding" (Doughty). The 1985 statement declares the Whooping Crane the property of both nations. Thus a question was answered which had been rumbling around ever since Josephine (U.S.-born) and Crip (Canadian-born) went to live in the New Orleans Zoo and to produce young.

Shortly after the 1954 discovery of the Whooping Cranes summering in Canada's Wood Buffalo Park, Canadian and U.S. biologists began to work together even more closely, planing back and forth from Canada to the U.S. just as the Whooping Crane, the species upon which they still exert much energy in preserving, does each spring and fall.

The scientists carried with them — aboard helicopter, single engine plane, or jet — a kind of renewal in a package. They bore with them in specially designed cases, the great white-winged bird's rare packet of genetic material: the speckled ovate eggs of the Whooping Crane.

Birds' eggs are like their shell, one of the most beautiful things on the planet. A person doesn't really know a bird until he can find its nest. Birds hide their nests so well that if you find an egg, it proves you know the bird and its habits.

VLADIMIR FLINT
Russian Biologist working with ICF to save the Siberian Crane, 1996

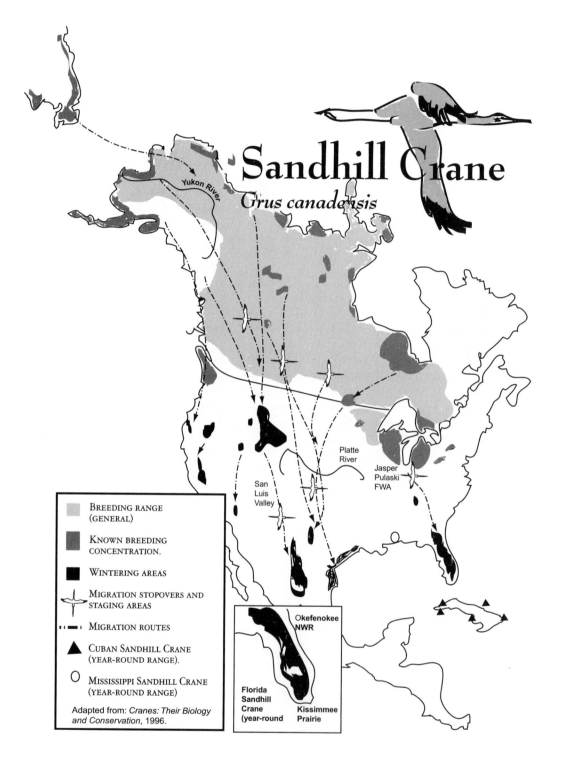

Sandhill Crane
Grus canadensis

Yukon River

Platte River

San Luis Valley

Jasper Pulaski FWA

BREEDING RANGE (GENERAL)

KNOWN BREEDING CONCENTRATION.

WINTERING AREAS

MIGRATION STOPOVERS AND STAGING AREAS

MIGRATION ROUTES

CUBAN SANDHILL CRANE (YEAR-ROUND RANGE).

MISSISSIPPI SANDHILL CRANE (YEAR-ROUND RANGE)

Adapted from: *Cranes: Their Biology and Conservation*, 1996.

Okefenokee NWR

Florida Sandhill Crane (year-round

Kissimmee Prairie

136

A Very Large Array
of Cranes

Except for the workings of the brain,
no other phenomenon
in the living world is as miraculous
and awe-inspiring as the development
of a new adult from a fertilized egg.

ERNST MAYR

This is Biology, 1997

A January Morning: Above the Southwest

Over Kansas aboard a Southwest Airlines jet bound for Albuquerque, I look down through the crystalline plexiglass window at the winter landscape skimming below. As we head straight west over broad buff and tan Kansas plains and cross the eastern edge of the Rockies, we'll intersect with one of the Sandhill Crane's traditional flightpaths. Connecting with it, the jet will bear south, passing above the Sangre de Cristo Mountains, the mountains the Spanish called "Blood of Christ" for their red dawn and sunset hues. Then we will be above the San Luis Valley, a major stop-off for Cranes migrating north or south, and where the Monte Vista National Wildlife Refuge spreads its Crane welcome in the lush valley.

The valley is edged on the west by distant big-shouldered mountains called the San Juan, but which the Spanish explorer Don Juan Bautista De Anza thought of as the *Sierra de las Grullas*, "the mountain range of the Cranes." The San Luis Valley from a Landsat Satellite photo looks somewhat like a cosmic egg held in the vise of the two mountain ranges.

It was here in the San Luis Valley where "the great river" the Rio Grande flows, beginning at its source farther north in Colorado and hurrying southward to bifurcate New Mexico and then curving eastward to form the border of Texas/Mexico, that the initial experiment in breeding Cranes in captivity was carried on.

"But things did not go well," as Robin Doughty and other sources will tell you. The primary reason was the Whooping Crane Recovery Program was under-funded in those early days, and Monte Vista did not even have enough facilities to house or to incubate the precious Crane eggs. Scientists began the experimentation at Monte Vista with the hope that the abundant Sandhills captured from the wild flocks stopping off there on migration would prove to rear their chicks suitably enough in captivity that they could be released into the wild.

The eventual goal was to study the possibility of Sandhill parents rearing Whooper chicks placed in their nests, a procedure called "cross-fostering." But the program was moved to Patuxent Wildlife Research Center near Laurel, Maryland where there were more facilities. With an

Pictograph of Cranes in flight found at Nogales Cliffhouse, near Llaves, New Mexico, *perhaps 10th century, (drawing by Stuart Peckham and cited by T.R. Frisbie).*

infusion of government funding behind it, and with George Gee beginning work there, the program of breeding Cranes in captivity began to progress at Patuxent.

Still loyal to Monte Vista and the San Luis Valley, however, the wild Cranes, particularly the Sandhills of the Rocky Mountain Population and a few Whoopers, stop off.

How the Whoopers began to migrate there and farther on to Bosque del Apache National Wildlife Refuge is a story which I'll tell further along.

At Bosque in the fall and each spring in the San Luis Valley, the human populace turns out in force to celebrate the Cranes' appearance with a Crane Festival. In Colorado, people from nearby Alamosa are proud to sport an enameled pin on lapel or dress. It is a miniature image of a Whooping Crane standing on what at first appears to be a brown rock, but on closer inspection turns out to be a giant potato, an important produce of the Valley as is the barley which entices the Cranes.

One of the many participants and leaders in the Crane Festival in Colorado is Donna Kingery who is an example of the dedicated "amateur," and amateurism in the root meaning of "devoted attention" such as that of the Michigan dentist Dr. Lawrence Walkinshaw's "amateur" status. For Donna Kingery has long served the world of Cranes. Since the 1970s she has kept a finger on the pulsing population numbers of Crane migration. From her office as bookkeeper in her husband George's contracting business, she receives phone calls from Crane spotters all over the Valley. When she finds out where they are, she's out in the green fields at once, binoculars in hand for a Crane count — gray-brown and white ones, too.

Donna Kingery's fervent devotion to the Cranes has earned her the title of "Crane Lady" given to her by the folks in the Valley. For she not only keeps logs of the Crane's numbers, their arrivals and departures, but she has also fought a good fight for Crane welfare. In doing so, she has involved the energy and support of her husband George, who documented her count with photographs, and her son Tanner.

In the 1980s, Donna and Tanner, then age twelve, became concerned then distressed at the deaths of Cranes which they discovered beneath power lines. A major nemesis to all large flying birds is power lines strung across the continent. Consequently, mother and son walked "three miles of power lines from Road 35 and 102 to the Rio Grande River, keeping charts of dead birds which they found, cataloging twenty-nine Sandhills and two Whoopers as a result of hitting powerlines" (*The Monte Vista Journal*, Wednesday, April 23, 1984). And when Donna witnessed the hard death of the Whooping Crane "Ida" as a result of striking a powerline, she gathered up her son's mortality statistics, and, armed like Robert Porter Allen with his Whooping Crane "Kill Records," headed for the offices of the Electric Power Company.

Here the story goes on in Donna Kingery's own words: "I decided right then and there that the Power Company was going to bury the lines. I went to their offices and asked to see the 'boss.' I told him the whole story. He called in a Public Relations man, and, after I calmed down, they suggested I write a letter explaining the problem to a higher up in the regional office. I left there thinking they just blew it off, and I'd never get anywhere."

If these balls were strung on wires near flight path of Cranes, mortality rates could be reduced by 80 per cent.

But Donna and Tanner did not stop with a letter. They enlisted local folk and some illustrious wildlife biologists such as Roderick Drewien at Grays Lake, Idaho and John Lewis of the USFWS, both men steeped in Crane lore. To make an endless paperwork story short, the Electric Power Company amazingly was listening. Donna received an official letter from them: they were "looking into the problem." And finally, the Power Company agreed to take the static lines down from the section most hazardous to the Cranes. For anyone who has ever attempted to communicate with the fortress of officials behind a public utility — and who hasn't in this technological age — the fact that the Power Company actually responded, is a victory for the Cranes effected by two individuals — Donna Kingery and twelve year old Tanner — and it is nothing short of miraculous. And the two thousand or so Sandhills and the twelve Whoopers who made the Valley the miracle of their "temporary" home, were at least no longer at risk from some powerlines, but of course not all. There would be other deaths of Cranes caught on powerlines high up and barbed wire low down.

Helicopter and Helix

Almost simultaneously with the Whooping Cranes' Canadian nesting area discovery by helicopter in the field, another major breakthrough in biological science occurred in the laboratory. It was a discovery so far-reaching that even with many advances we are only now beginning to explore and to apply some of its possibilities.

In 1953, the model of DNA (*deoxyribonucleic acid*) constructed from and based upon the x-ray crystallographs of Rosalind Franklin was made by James Watson and Francis Crick thus revealing a most basic structure in the language of life.

Knowing that structure of DNA, says Sir John Maddox, gave us "the repository of the recipe by means of which a single fertilized egg in a sexually reproductive organism can develop into a fully functioning adult; what is called ontogeny has at last been unambiguously brought within the bonds of rational inquiry."

Consequently, through this genetic mapping of the "double helix," a chromosomal double spiral of different nucleotides assigned an alphabet of four letters: A (*adenine*); T (*thymine*); G (*guanine*); and C (*cytosine*) a vast new Alphabet would open up not only to avian scientists but to all of the Life Sciences, and, indeed, potentially affect all life on the planet.

With the DNA discovery also eventually came a shake-up in the classical and traditional taxonomy, the "System of Nature" by which living creatures are separated into species, genera, families, and ultimately the kingdoms of Animal and Plant.

For example, although the two species of North American Cranes, the Whooper and Sandhill, share many behavioral and geographical characteristics, they are not as clearly related to one another as others in the family Gruidae. It was genetic testing which informed biologists that the Whooping Crane is a nearer relative of the Red-Crowned Crane, *Grus japonensis*, found in Japan and China, than the Sandhill and Whooper are to one another (Archibald). However, it is because the two North Americans share so many parenting habits which had been studied that the Sandhills were thought to be the best and most obtainable Cranes for foster parents. As we will see farther

Japanese clan crest.

along, scientists acted upon this principle: the survival of the Whooping Crane, even after its nesting discovery, appeared more imperiled over time.

Each year Whooping Crane nests were censused by biologists flying in a helicopter over Wood Buffalo. Each year numerous twin chicks were duly recorded, and each year, if young arrived in Aransas with their parents, they were generally a single fledgling. One cause could be that Cranes do not wait until all eggs are hatched to incubate them, as say, Swans do. Consequently, the first laid egg hatches out a chick dominant over its fellow nestling. The last laid of the two does not always survive if it hatches out. Thus biologists hit upon a solution which they would act upon beginning in 1967.

The solution was to take one of the two eggs from the nest of the wild white Cranes in Canada, a concerted and hazardous effort. Up until 1967, only injured birds spotted below in Wood Buffalo or on migration were taken to Patuxent Wildlife Research Center where in 1975 the Whooping Crane "Dawn" appeared as the first to be hatched from parents living at the breeding facility.

Also at Patuxent was one particular mighty Crane who began his contribution to Whooping Crane survival. Canus was the first white Crane to arrive in the San Luis Valley in over many centuries.

And he came there by a devious route. But evidence of the Whoopers' long-ago presence in the Valley and the general region of the Southwest is apparent in the images depicted by ancient tribes.

There are some petroglyph images which anthropologists have discovered incised on rock. Several of them in this region of Colorado, New Mexico, and Arizona indicate the white bird's possible presence in a broad region of the Southwest.

Anthropologists who study the ways of humans say the early humans studied the animals, and they knew their ways better than those of

Petroglyph from Colorado—note Crane in lower left corner, from *Picture Writing of the American Indians*.

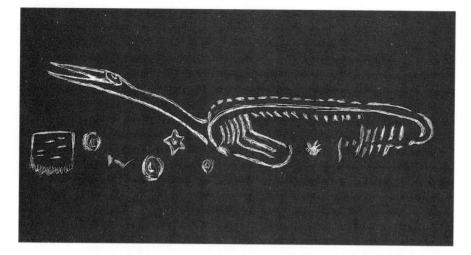

their own species, *Homo sapiens*. In order to hunt, these ancient peoples had to know how to walk in the animals' footsteps.

Thus an animal's image such as the Whooping Crane's scratched on the roof of a cave in Rio Grande National Forest is put there to convey an entirely different message than say an explorer's —

Crane image on cave in Rio Grande National Forest— conjecture is that it was pecked in stone around 2000 years ago *(redrawn from photo)*.

Spanish or English — depiction of a Crane. As was John White's, a sixteenth century English explorer and settler of Roanoke, who made a drawing of the "Virginia Crane" to send back to Sir Walter Raleigh in a report on animals in the New World.

But whether or not the Whooping Crane's image incised on rock is there for reasons of ceremony or for a clan mark, or to record its appearance, is impossible to say for those of us incapable of perceiving the world as did these ancient peoples. Nevertheless, the presence of the Whooping Crane images could give us pause to wonder if knowledge and awareness by the cave artist signifies the great bird's visit here on a migratory passage through the Valley.

In *Picture Writing of the American Indians* by Garrick Mallery published in 1893 by the Smithsonian Institution appears a drawing by its discoverer in this area of Colorado and it is a marvelous procession of figures. Humans, animals, and strange flying creatures were depicted. This could be the ancient version of the Crane Festival in the Valley because the entire procession pecked into the rock appears to be presided over by a giant bird, a Crane, certainly by its size, it could be a Whooper. A closer guess as to the meaning of this petroglyph is that it probably represents one of the numerous migrations of not only animals but also humans into this region thousands of year ago.

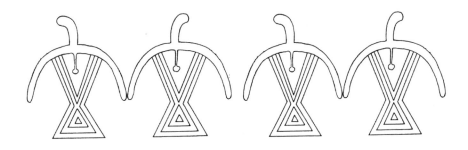

SANDHILL CRANE

Sandhill crane, do you ache?
You Shy from man at dusk. They hunted you.
They killed the whooper, your brighter cousin.
Now you fly
Along the meanders. Gray wings spread as you rise.
Vast and aching before you hide in the needlegrass.
You shy even from the horses who run the stone hills,
Manes flying.
Trailed by plumes of phosphorescent dust.
Knife edges of sunlight glint upon their throats.

RON ROGERS
(Cherokee)
courtesy of Joseph Bruchac

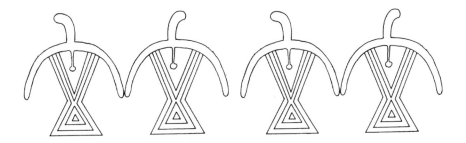

CANada + US =
"CANUS" the Whooper

But Canus the first white Crane to arrive in Monte Vista in modern times didn't make it on his own wing. He was picked up from Wood Buffalo in Canada by two wildlife biologists aboard a helicopter: S. Novakowski and Ernie Kuyt spotted him below, an injured bird incapable of flying. Via a set of various recuperative efforts chronicled by Jerome J. Pratt, we find Canus first at Patuxent, treated for disease and injury. Thus, revivified like a Phoenix, Canus was flown to Monte Vista to join the initial captive breeding program.

However, more misadventures occurred — those which can only happen to a young gawky Crane. Canus was returned to Patuxent. There he became a valuable source for artificial insemination. According to Patuxent's George Gee, Canus still is. A long exponent of captive breeding, Jerome J. Pratt comments: "If it hadn't been for the human helping hand this bird [Canus] would have died obscurely in the wilderness."

With artificial insemination (AI) developed for Cranes at Patuxent by George Gee, you may have a captive pair bred to one another artificially, and you may have a fertile egg or two, but the captive chick reared from the egg by humans is indelibly imprinted on the caregiver, the provider of food. So you have to solve the riddle of how to rear the chick away from human intrusion and imprinting. This trait was studied by Konrad Lorenz, a Nobel Laureate who worked with waterfowl, specifically the Greylag Geese.

Lorenz describes the behavior of the young geese "imprinted" on a caregiver as evidencing "all the behavior patterns a young bird would normally show toward a parent."

A famous film sequence often included in TV Nature specials shows Lorenz, a bearded man walking along a path, dutifully followed by a chain of young geese walking single file behind him. They are goslings imprinted on him as their surrogate "Mother Goose."

The trait of imprinting has been used to advantage recently in experiments to "teach" first Canada Geese to migrate by imprinting them on the sound of an ultralight plane's motor and its pilot Bill Lishman, sometimes called "Father Goose."

A flock of ducks followed St. Colman, St Brendan the Navigator—

a pet crow,

and St Colum Cille—

a pet Crane

SEUMAS MCMANUS
The Story of the Irish Race

Sketch of mask:
Kwakwakawaku
by MUNGO MARTIN
Northwest Coast
representing
"Supernatural Sandhill Crane."
(*Gilcrease Museum, 1998*)

In a later 1997 experiment, Cranes including young Whoopers, followed Kent Clegg aboard an ultralight, a migration of man and birds flying from Idaho to Bosque del Apache National Wildlife Reserve.

Another scientist, Dave Ellis of Patuxent, has successfully imprinted Cranes on a truck's engine. In all the experiments, with Nature's few exceptions, the Canadas or the Sandhills followed aloft behind the pilot or driver as willingly as the goslings followed Konrad Lorenz afoot.

Birds born fully capable of seeing and hearing, as are for example the Goose's gosling, the Swan's cygnet, and the Crane's chicks are called "precocial," and each shares this trait of bonding with a caregiver — human or goose — and in the case of Cranes they become so attached to a human caregiver, a parent to the bird, that they become jealous guardians of the human. A Crane bonded so to a human companion will not only keep other Cranes away but also other humans.

Field biologists faced a vast dilemma when in 1961 no young Cranes accompanied their parents from Canada to Texas. The attempt to preserve the Whooping Crane seemed to be back to square one. At thirty-two Cranes, the adult population of wild Cranes stood exactly at the same number it had when Robert Porter Allen of the Audubon Society

Young Brolga Crane, *Grus rubicunda*. The Brolga, also known as the Australian Crane, live in northern and eastern Australia as well as southern New Guinea. Though prefering to nest in shallow freshwater marshes and wet meadows, they also can be found in brackish coastal wetlands. They are the only Crane to have a salt gland (located at the corner of the eyes) which allows them to expel excess salt. The ability to adapt to a wide variety of habitats makes the Brolga Crane less susceptible to problems which affect other Crane species. Brolga populations are stable, but estimates vary widely from 20,000 to 100,000 birds.

and the USFWS team together with Canadians first began the project in 1947.

Not only did the wild population seem to be at a standstill in the 1960s, but a great tragedy, a major setback also occurred in the slender captive Crane breeding program, the death of the only breeding female, Josephine.

Like the hurricane winds wiping out most of the wild resident Crane population in Louisiana in 1940, ultimately leaving only Josephine as their living representative, another hurricane swept up the Gulf, heading directly toward New Orleans where Josephine and her mate Crip lived and produced young. The year was 1965, and, by this time, the pair had produced over fifty eggs, some of them infertile. But from their vast production four young Cranes lived — George, Georgette, Pee Wee, and Pepper.

With the hurricane on its way — and this one had a name, Hurricane Betsy — the major priority of the Audubon Park Zoo was to safeguard the rare couple and their progeny.

Therefore, keepers, three keepers per Crane, escorted Josephine and Crip from their airy wire pens and guided them into a permanent building. It took three keepers in attendance, one holding the bill clamped shut and one keeper each holding a wing.

The building where they took these Cranes, called the "giraffe of birddom" for their lofty height by natural scientists, was ironically the Giraffe House. The keepers left them in the long and presumably dark corridor. Their four offspring were dispersed to other buildings as a preservation safeguard.

Before Hurricane Betsy hit, all the humans holed up in the Administration Building.

The storm finally wore itself out after landfall, and it began to drop off at midnight. The Zoo workers had to hack their way through fallen trees, and it wasn't until dawn that they could reach the buildings housing the Cranes. "All the brick buildings were intact," says Faith McNulty whose work is the source for this chronicle, "but the once lovely park was a ghastly tangle of roots and branches of fallen trees."

The two adults Josephine and Crip and their four children had survived the storm.

As soon as possible the keepers returned the Cranes to their wire pens. Despite the devastation to the plants and trees, all the larger animals seemed to be well, even though crews working near the pens were still hacking away at fallen vegetation.

Possibly to survey the damage, a helicopter hovered over the zoo. Its whirlybird rotors and the roar of its motor severely frightened the already stressed and fearful birds.

But for Josephine, captured from the wild long ago by men in helicopters, the nemesis in the sky was too much.

She gave a mighty and powerful forward thrust to her body, lifting her great pinioned wings in a clear attempt to fly away from the peril overhead, a natural reaction of any wild bird.

Thus, she smashed into the wire enclosure with all her might and fell back. But she tried again and again, beating her mighty wings like a butterfly in a glass bell jar, until her "wing bones were rubbed raw." Exhausted, she, like the storm, subsided.

The keepers, probably stressed as well from enduring the hurricane, looked in and guessed that she "suffered no serious injury." But the next morning the great Louisiana Crane who had lived twenty-four years of a captive, but productive life, was dead.

But Crip, her mate, survived the storm as did the four young. Later on, they were sexed by scientist Roxy Laybourne. George, Pepper, and Georgette were found to be males and Pee Wee the lone female. Consequently, there was backpeddling on the names and George became "Angus" and Georgette merely "George."

Luckily, as it happened there was another captive wild female to take Josephine's place. Rosie resided at the San Antonio Zoo after she was rescued from injuries and captured at Aransas. Thus Angus was sent off to San Antonio to pair with Rosie. No luck. Then Angus's father, a proven producer was sent to pair with Rosie. What happened at their assignation in San Antonio will provide us with an extraordinary tale of the survival of a famous captive Crane.

Melodious is the crane in the marshlands of Drium du Thren. She cannot save her nestling, the red fox has torn them.

COLLOQUY OF THE ANCIENTS
Irish, 12th century

Red Sky at Dawn

Albuquerque is fortunate for its many rich sights, "Old Town" the Spanish Adobe Square near the Rio Grande for one. Another is provided by its location on the flight path of the Cranes. In fall and spring, great flying wedges of Sandhills stream above the town.

Whooping Cranes may also be spotted, flying singly, the white sparkle of their feathers scudding among the darker gray-brown Cranes, their fellow migrants.

Although I've been to New Mexico many times before this, I've generally preferred to drive here. Driving from the east, I reach the border of Texas and New Mexico, and a rich wonder falls over me as I pass the sign "Bienvenidos" welcoming the traveler to this "land of enchantment."

Now on the ground and in a van beside Kay, a fellow Audubon Society member, we head straight south to the town of Socorro — and ultimately, nearby Bosque del Apache National Wildlife Refuge, just a little south and east of the town. Bosque, the "woods of the Apache tribe" and the town the Spanish called "Help" or "Nuestra Senora de Perpetuo Socorro," Our Lady of Perpetual Help. This was also the name of the mission they established there to "harvest the souls" of the Indian people, the Piro, who came to the Spaniards' aid when the soldiers arrived exhausted and starved.

The highway takes us along the Rio Grande, lying always to our left. A morning mist hangs above the willows and cottonwoods hugging their silvery shapes to the serpentine course of the river, a great part of which is hidden underground, a deep subterranean flow.

New Mexico is like that. Deep secret currents of the past, present, and future are surprises to be found by the traveler, many of them in plain sight such as the frequent archeological sites of ancient peoples or modern technological wonders such as radio astronomy. Yet below and upon this spectacular landscape are many riddles — both ancient and modern — or futuristic. Some could be the stuff of

Acoma Pueblo seed pot from New Mexico showing the contemporary use of a Crane motif.

science fiction, such as Roswell, where extraterrestrials are said to have crash-landed.

The first time I came here, scores of years ago — also a passenger in a car driven by a knowledgeable driver, it was a working trip from which I derived great pleasure and many new experiences.

Just out of college, I was employed by Philbrook Art Museum which houses a splendid Native American art collection. And I was traveling as assistant to Indian Art Curator Dorothy Field (later Maxwell). Even then Dorothy and her father Clark Field were known for their Amerindian art collection and research.

I was to assist Dorothy in her special researching of Pueblo Indian pottery and basketry. And, I didn't realize then, but it was to be an experience which would "imprint" me for life — with everything from landscapes of red cliffs and mesas to the half-feather design on the San Ildefonso Pueblo potter Maria Martinez's work. Although I was very young then, I was aware that I was in a strange new/old land.

Located at the northern edge of the Chihuahuan desert, the heart of the Bosque del Apache National Wildlife Refuge is 12,900 acres of moist bottomlands. 3,800 acres are active Rio Grande floodplain, while on the other 9,100 acres water is diverted to create extensive wetlands, farmlands, and riparian forests. The remaining areas are the arid foothills and mesas which rise to the Chupadera Mountains on the west and the San Pascual Mountains on the east.

First Glimpse

"Look over there," Kay says, pointing toward her left.

Far to the east, their long skeins mirroring the flow of the Rio Grande as it meanders southward, thousands of Snow Geese flow in a dense flock through the roseate dawn sky. I lift my camera to my eye.

Kay slows the van and pulls off on the pebble-strewn shoulder. I'm in luck. I'm traveling with a birder — patient and understanding of that great passion to record, if not on film but only through the eye, the overwhelming sight. She leans back and lowers her window. The high clear mountain air of New Mexico streams in and around us. It is my "decisive moment" — and the camera clicks.

"Just wait," Kay, an experienced birder and a biologist, says. "I've been to Bosque before, and I warrant you that there will be birding sights you'll never forget."

"I can hardly wait to see the Cranes," I say.

"You'll see the Cranes," says Kay, turning back onto the road. "Tomorrow you'll see thousands of Cranes — and Snow Geese too at first light."

I pick up the road map beside me on the seat and study the territory. Heretofore, most of my New Mexico ramblings have been in the northern section above Highway 40, the old Route 66 which transects the state marking off north and south.

This is a comparatively new territory for me. Highway 25, the road we're following to Socorro, plunges straight down, southward. Paralleling the Rio Grande, it flows to the Mexican border, where Texas touches New Mexico. A distribution map of Sandhills will show you that the Cranes too follow this river thoroughfare. And, although thousands of them halt at Bosque, many go on dispersing into Arizona and Mexico.

Like Aransas Wildlife Refuge in Texas, established in 1937 to protect the Whooper, Bosque del Apache National Wildlife Refuge was established two years later to protect "the endangered Sandhill" and many other migratory birds as well.

Numbering now between thirty thousand and forty thousand birds, the Greater Sandhill population at that time was down to "less than a thousand. " Several years after the Refuge was established only "seven-

teen wintered there" (Maurer). Besides a few Whoopers, other Sandhill subspecies are here too.

Cranes winging home to Bosque del Apache, New Mexico.

A diagram of the fifty-seven thousand one hundred ninety-one acre Refuge appears somewhat like a trapezoid, and, unintentionally, of course, the roads of the tour loop appear very like the shape of a great Crane's head and bill.

Beneath the nearby river and below the highway we travel along is part of what geologists call the "Rio Grande Rift." The great cleft in the earth begins in Colorado with the Rio Grande's source, runs through the San Luis Valley into New Mexico, through Taos, Santa Fe, Albuquerque, and now where we are and on south to Mexico.

The concept of this great southwestern rift was not really "recognized until the late 1970s," says geologist Walter Sullivan. It is a rift marking a thirty-two million year old cleavage in the earth "where forces within the earth apparently have tried unsuccessfully to tear the continent apart." Other major examples of such rifts are the East African Rift and the rift in Siberia.

We pass a highway sign marking a turnoff to the town of Belen and the State Wildlife Refuge. From Belen and south to Socorro, Sullivan says, "recent seismic soundings [have detected] what appears to be a great body of molten rock at least seventeen miles long and twelve miles wide lying a dozen miles beneath the rift."

There are few roads branching off from Highway 25. But if we would happen to swing off eastward at Socorro, we would soon come to the Trinity Site, "ground zero" where the atomic bomb first mushroomed into the sky — "not open to visitors in the winter."

The site obviously was chosen by physicists from Los Alamos to the north because of its isolation. Interestingly enough in one of the odd convergences of language — especially when you remember physicist J. Robert Oppenheimer's saying as he watched the first experimental atomic bomb flash upward into the sky in 1945 — "we have become death" — the Spanish explorers much earlier called this area "Jornada del Muerto. " To denote a day's Journey on horseback through the deathlike desert landscape the Spanish called it the "Journey of Death." The Camino Real, their Royal Highway, is now Highway 25, and it veers away from the river which it eventually rejoins and parallels.

Radio telescopes of the *Very Large Array* search deep space near Magdelena, New Mexico.

On the other hand, if we go westward instead from Socorro along Highway 60, we'd come to the Plains of San Agustin, created by the Rio Grande Rift, where the "Very Large Array" is located. There, radio astronomers are observing life — not life on this planet — but life that might exist in outer space.

Home of the National Radio Astronomy Observatory, this surreal landscape is strung with twenty-seven enormous white antennas. Weighing some two hundred thirty-five tons, they look like gargantuan television satellite dishes which, from a distance, appear like white beads on a string. These antennas are so huge that, to change their

orientation they are installed on railroad car size wheeled platforms to move them along a Y-shaped track. Here, astronomers from assorted universities take turns not only listening for life messages relayed hopefully from outer space, but they are also visualizing deep space images through radio waves bouncing into their computers. They may watch such distant wonders materialize on their screens as a supernova remnant, the birth of a star, or the flowing gases of the Horsehead Nebula.

Entering the town of Socorro, we join our fellow Audubon Society members who wait for us in a cluster of birders in front of the Vagabond Hotel. Like Geoffrey Chaucer's medieval pilgrims on a pilgrimage or more aptly his *Parliament of Fowls*, we are, for the human species, a mixed flock. Each of us represent much diversity in the species *Homo sapiens sapiens*: Lab technicians, Teachers, Plumbers, Pilots, Construction Workers, and young adults just starting their birding forays as well as a seasoned birder like Dee. By the time Dee hung up her binoculars and stopped counting, she had garnered over seven hundred North American species of birds on her Life List — a master birder.

Some ten cars in a caravan led by two competent birders, begin the last leg of our birding pilgrimage to Bosque. On the way, and the way is

A Whooping Crane has been painted as part of a wall mural on a kiva ceremonial chamber at Pottery Mound ruins, located 45 miles southwest of Albuquerque along the Puerco River. *Maxwell Museum of Anthropology, University of New Mexico (as cited by T.R. Frisbie)*

a halting one for birdwatchers, there are frequent stops for the unusual birds, clearly sighted on this sunny winter day.

When you see a cluster of cars and vans pulled off the road ahead, you know at once there is something special in the way of birddom for you to see. The first pause is just a slowdown to allow a covey of Gambel's Quail to skitter across the road. These little fellows have a piquant beauty to them, compact little Quail bodies with a curlicue topknot that looks like a doodle. Then there is a clear halt for a Marsh Hawk on a desert tree, next a yellow headed blackbird.

This is a birders' paradise: landbirds to shorebirds, neo-tropical migrants to desert rarities such as the Roadrunner, the bird on the city of Socorro's logo. Finally, the familiar flying Goose etched on the brown wood of the U.S. Fish and Wildlife Service's Refuge sign. Along the halting way, I see an occasional echelon of two or three Sandhills in the high blue sky. But now, as we enter the Refuge, well now, there are Sandhills everywhere — some shuttling overhead right past my camera lens, some pausing in the marsh to feed on protein creatures. These migrant birds know a good thing when they find it, and they have found Bosque in great numbers.

With "extensive wetlands" diverted from the waters of the Rio Grande to create marshes and ponds, the Refuge is overlooked by foothills and mesas rising to blue brown Chupadero Mountains on the west.

Bald Eagle in a tree at Bosque del Apache.

To the east are the pale blue brown rippling peaks of the San Pasqual Mountains. Desert/marsh/lowlands/highlands — every kind of habitat a bird could want — a "green Oasis surrounded by arid desert," all embraced by distant mountains.

Another stop ahead. Something really good. On a Cottonwood tree near a blue ditch of fresh water, a single mature Bald Eagle peers down quizzically at a platoon of Sandhills feeding in the long Tamarind grass.

My first glimpse of the Sandhills was years ago on a windswept Padre Island in Texas. Driving along, I turned my head to see a field of what looked to my inexperienced eye like a herd of four-footed animals — possibly sheep. When you see Sandhills busy feeding, in long buff-brown grass, you see only the arc topping their feathered bodies showing above the tips of grass.

No wonder the English collective noun for Cranes was once a "herd" of Cranes and the young Cranes were called "colts" in the time before they disappeared from England. With their long necks and legs out of sight, the cranes appear more like four-legged animals than great two-legged birds. But, of course, the Eagle isn't fooled in the least.

Sandhill Cranes foraging at Bosque del Apache—first scratching the dirt with their claws, then probing the ground with their bills. Crane bills are very sharp and sturdy, useful even on frozen ground. With serrated edges, they can grasp slippery food like worms, snakes, or frogs.

In 1997, when Pilot Kent Clegg was traversing the Rocky Mountain flyway leading aloft in his ultralight plane a flock of imprinted Cranes behind him in the air, he lost one of the airborne Cranes to an Eagle which hurled the hapless bird right out of the sky. It would be inadvisable for a Marsh Hawk to attack a "warlike Crane." For our mighty national bird the Eagle, it's another story indeed.

Farther along, just as the road loops toward the western mountains, the entire caravan halts. Everyone out of the cars. Spotting scopes in place.

Before us is an absolute miracle, a sweeping panorama of wild birds, upland birds, marsh feeders, shorebirds. In the foreground, scores of Sandhills, unobscured by tall grass, poke their long bills into the ground. Making holes in dry earth, their bills disappear up to the eyes, leaving only their red crowns in view. Underneath the surface they are searching for tubers, but, like the Platte River area, there's plenty of corn stalks for them planted there by the Bosque Refuge staff and a troop of volunteers.

Behind the feeding Cranes, a magnificent white band of Snow Geese salts the brown land. Among them, a tall shape, its long white neck and body clearly recognizable, is a lone Whooping Crane, one of the four which followed Kent Clegg here.

On the ground in front of the band of Snow Geese, two predatory dark shapes of bird share the white body of an unlucky Snow Goose.

When back
to Nile
from war
with Pygmies
Come
the Cranes,
the waterbirds
are meat
for every one.

CLAUDIUS
Roman Poet
395-404 A.D.

Through the long range lens, I see clearly that the shapes are two imma-ture Bald Eagles.

And because I have the camera raised and steady, the decisive mo-ment comes: at first only a soaring dark fleck in the sky, then as if re-leased from the blue mountain's eyrie in the far distance behind the feeding Snow Geese, a Bald Eagle, its white head now clearly visible, swoops on the unwary flock of Geese — "And like a thunderbolt he falls."

The Geese rise in one quivering long white band of Geese. Their black wingtips scarcely apparent, they beat as one solid ribbon of white. Through these thousand birds, the dark Eagle drops. Snatching one goose from the air, the great raptor plummets earthward, its prey held in its crooked talons.

Herding / Flocking

Numerous Eagles in winter may gather together to roost on trees. I have seen as many as thirty come into one area for roosting. But by day they are mostly solitary feeders — as are Hawks. But birds like Snow Geese and Sandhills, "birds of a feather," they "flock together" in enormous collections of birds.

When the great animal behaviorist Konrad Lorenz ponders this behavioral trait of flocking/herding animals, he first points to the disadvantages which he says are at least three: (1) the difficulty of finding sufficient food for so many animals in one place, (2) the impossibility of concealment when in great numbers — as are the Snow Geese, (3) the increased possibility of disease — avian cholera for one.

Then, if there are so many disadvantages, asks Lorenz, why do animals flock/herd together? A significant answer, he says, is that large numbers of animals make it difficult for a predator — such as the Eagle — to spot and keep track of one single animal, thus to separate it from the others.

Keen-eyed though the Eagle is, for the particular one I saw to snag a Snow Goose is a case of random luck. The Eagle could have made many tries before it caught one Goose. This single advantage for the herders/flockers provides the pressure for them to stay together. Consequently, the "gregarious" animals as opposed to the loners, not only stay together in great swarms/herds/flocks, but they also press together when alarmed — whenever there is a suspicion of a predator close at hand."

Furthermore, flockers may differ in their relationship to one another when in large collections. In only a few species, says Lorenz, for example "swans, wild geese and cranes, do mates or parents and children keep together in the big migrating flocks."

The Whooping Crane, not a big flocker as we have seen earlier, migrates and arrives at Aransas Wildlife Refuge in Texas in close family groups. But Sandhills, big flockers, try to maintain their family ties within large groups.

Seen on the hills at a distance [the Cranes] look like a force clad in pale grey with sentinels and outposts carefully placed at their flanks to give notice of an approaching enemy.

COLONEL CHESNEY,
English in Arabia (1860)

The Man with Three Homes
and a Thousand Cranes

*He goes
like a stalking Crane
when in the fields
he feeds on forlorn
grains which lie
upon the land,
with paces rare
he looks for seeds.*

BAPTISTA SPAGNUOLI
(1447-1516)

Two species of white geese arrive here before the Cranes come, the larger Snow Goose (*Chen caerulescens*) and the smaller Ross' Goose (*Chen rossii*). But the Sandhills wintering here at Bosque are of three different subspecies or forms, they travel three different distances to their breeding grounds, and they are three different sizes. The Lesser Sandhill (*Grus canadensis canadensis*) is the smallest of the Sandhills, standing about thirty-nine inches high. The Lessers come from the farthest away — their breeding range includes the distant edges of Alaska and even Siberia. The Canadian Sandhill (*Grus canadensis rowani*) the next in size, at seven inches or so taller than the Lesser, shares some of its breeding range with the Whooper (*Grus americana*) including Canada's Wood Buffalo and also much farther east, nesting areas near and south of Hudson's Bay. Some of the Canada Sandhills come here from Canada. The Greater Sandhill (*Grus canadensis tabida*) which nests from southern Oregon and northeast California all the way into Wisconsin and Michigan, disperses on different migratory pathways, some to the Atlantic, some to Texas. Most of these Greaters which come from Idaho, Wyoming, Montana and Utah are the Cranes making a stopover in Colorado's San Luis Valley, and they are part of the Rocky Mountain Population.

Grays Lake National Wildlife Refuge is where the story, like the Greaters' migration odyssey, begins. It is a story of the concerted attempt to re-introduce the Whooping Crane to the Rocky Mountain area. It is a project because of the heroic demands on human resources which has become almost a legendary one in Crane annals of the twentieth century. And it is a bold experiment. For there was no way for scientists to know or to factor in all the permutations of bringing together two different species of Cranes. And, again, totally new territory would be explored, for even though more than three decades had passed since Robert Porter Allen experimented with rearing a Whooping Crane chick, there was still very little known about the process — particularly in the wild.

The solitary Whooper we saw among the Snow Geese at Bosque is part of that story. Reared by foster parent Sandhills in Idaho, the tall white Crane represents the great hope biologists had of creating another wild migratory flock of Whoopers, and one migrating on a different corridor than of those Cranes of the Texas to Canada flyway — a safeguard finally agreed upon (or at least a kind of truce was made) between the wildness and the captive-rearing exponents.

The project answered for most of them the question of how to rear Whoopers under wild — not captive — conditions. Furthermore, it answered the question of how to propagate more Whooping Cranes so they could migrate; thus, in some ways the endeavor satisfied those who called out to intervene in preserving and protecting the slender Aransas/ Wood Buffalo populace from the ever-present endangerment such as a single disaster.

It all begins in 1975 when a young biologist from the University of Idaho contracted with the USFWS to head the Rocky Mountain Whooping Crane Recovery project.

Roderick C. Drewien had already spent some years making indepth studies of Sandhills, and he had completed his dissertation for his PhD: "Ecology of Rocky Mountain Greater Sandhills" in 1973.

Long before Drewien began his university studies, Elwood G. Bizeau began the study of Sandhill Cranes in their Idaho habitat. For, as Bizeau says when in college he had "sloshed around Grays Lake Marsh in the summer of 1949 and 1950, an inexperienced, but eager graduate student" marking every Crane nest he saw (Pratt). Bizeau continued to work with Drewien on the Whooping Crane project.

Even with help and with his own keen knowledge, Rod Drewien's task was an enormous one. It involved timing and close coordination with Canadian wildlife biologists. The Canadian team, headed by Ernie Kuyt (whom you saw earlier saving Canus from the marsh in Canada) would take one of the Whoopers customary two eggs from the nest in Wood Buffalo and then fly them to Grays Lake. Drewien in a boat or slogging on foot would replace both eggs removed from the Sandhill nest with Whooper egg substituted — and fingers crossed — the Sandhill parents would rear the Whooper chick as their own — which they did (Drewien, personal communication).

When it finally came time for the Sandhills to migrate, in October, the Whooping Crane, imprinted with its Sandhill foster parents, would learn the migratory route southward — a necessary lesson for Cranes, but not all birds. Some young birds migrate on their own. As for example some European examples, like the young of the European Swift (*Apus apus*) and the White Wagtail (*Motocalla alba*) migrate before the older birds even leave on migration (Waterman).

The issue in 1994 of these stamps by the United States Post Office marked international cooperation to save Cranes—Whooping Crane is native to North America, but Black-necked Crane is a rare breed found in Tibet and China.

Carved wooden
sculpture of a Crane
by PAUL NAGYOUALIK,
Inuit, *Baker Lake*.
*(photograph courtesy of
Gallery Indigena,
Stratford, Ontario, Canada)*

The Canadian and U.S. biologists agreed upon a method called "cross-fostering," and the Whoopers would be reared as wild birds. Consequently, they would not be imprinted on human caregivers as are captive-reared Cranes such as Josephine's and her mate Crip's offspring in the New Orleans Zoo.

The wild project was a dramatic and all-encompassing experiment, carefully prepared for by first taking eggs from a Whooper nest in Canada and then practicing putting an egg in a Sandhill's nest. This was just one of the tasks closely watched until the project should begin.

Not only was great care and study undertaken before the attempt to cross-foster was made, but there was also a realization that there would be certain risks to the human coordinators. Ernie Kuyt and his team would have to land a helicopter in the vast wilderness of Wood Buffalo, take the eggs — a single one from each far flung nest — and then fly them to Grays Lake.

On the Grays Lake end of the line, Drewien would have to take his chances with warlike Sandhills defending their nests.

But there was indeed in Rod Drewien the kind of "Crane Man" the program needed. Biologists, aviculturists, and the increasingly concerned public as well were calling for someone who could "think like a Crane" — and if anyone could, it was Drewien who knew every individual quirk and trait of each member of the nesting Sandhill families.

For recordkeeping, Drewien would equal Lawrence Walkinshaw and for Crane astute observation in the field he would in many ways parallel Robert Porter Allen (who died in 1963). Drewien had observed and recorded "close details about the reliability of specific pairs" of Sandhills. A valuable knowledge for their suitability as parents (Doughty).

When Donna Kingery discovered Whooping Crane "Ida" dead by impact with a powerline in Colorado's San Luis Valley, she called Rod Drewien for help and further background information to assist in her battle to induce the Electric Power Company to take down some of the hazardous lines — and he gave it. For he had watched "Ida" — giving her a number 76-15 since she was hatched by foster parent Sandhills at Grays Lake.

And Drewien knew from unfortunate experience what may happen to a Crane through those random and haphazard impacts with lines and wires — on poles high in the air or strung between fence posts lower down. The barbed wire could catch a low-flying Crane and sometimes kill it instantly on impact.

For someone who has devoted many years of his life to Cranes, Drewien was in for many victories — successes which could lift anyone's spirits, and he would contribute much new knowledge in the ways not only of the Sandhill but also of the Whooping Crane — arguably one of the most heavily and intensely studied of birds ever — and still called a "flagship bird" by the USFWS's Tom Stehn who also knows their ways.

Drewien would face many losses as well. Those ambivalent YES/NO answers Nature gives to any human experimenting in her realm.

One yes-success for Drewien was number 75-1, the Whooper he called "Miracles" for the white Crane's miraculous escapes from every sort of predicament a young Whooping Crane could find to get in.

Miracles was given the number 75-1 by Ernie Kuyt when he labeled the eggs after picking them up at Wood Buffalo. The identification was the year (75) and the number for each egg. Thus Miracles was one of the first eggs to be picked up out of the fourteen. Of the fourteen, Miracles was one of five who survived to fledge. Watched over and protected, guided away from dangerous dogs or the intrusion of cattle by his wary Sandhill parents, Miracles outlived all the other foster-reared birds of his hatch year, migrating successfully from Idaho to New Mexico.

By this time in Canada, Kuyt and Drewien had begun color-marking young Whoopers with a legband denoting their year of hatching. Some young chicks also wore radio transmitters so that humans could track them. This procedure enabled biologists to follow the welfare and whereabouts of the young Cranes which can sometimes, like human teenagers with car keys in hand, begin to explore new territory away from their parents.

Consequently, with Drewien also following this procedure with the Idaho Crane chicks, he was able to learn much of the errant travels of Miracles and his cohort fledglings.

Hide painting of Crane, *Abenaki,* East Coast.

To track the Whooper fledglings migrating with their Sandhill parents, Drewien lived as Robin Doughty says "in three different homes": he made his base at Grays Lake, then traveling southward following the Cranes for their month-long stopover, he lived in San Luis Valley. Finally, he went onward to Bosque del Apache National Wildlife Refuge — the Cranes' and Drewien's wintertime stopover.

After Miracles and the rest of the 1975 cohort fledgling Whoopers left Idaho, and Drewien followed them south, it wasn't too long that he discovered Miracles had gotten himself in a perilous situation — one which would call for a certain miraculous and charmed life if the young Crane were to survive his first year.

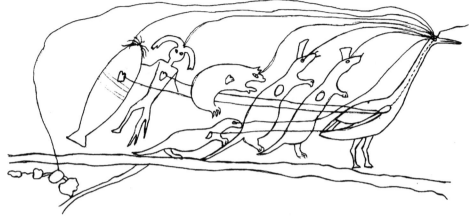

The Crane as Cheiftain of the Ojibwa animal clans.

The Creator of all things sent two cranes to search for a perfect place to rest.
When they found that place, they were to fold their wings and wait.
First, they flew to the prairies and tasted Bison meat.
The meat was good, but they saw very few Bison.
Then they flew to the forest where many four-legged animals lived.
Their meat was good, but for many days, they saw no more animals.
Then they flew to the Great Lakes, and they landed on the shore.
Every day their were plenty of fish for them to eat.
So they folded their wings and waited.
They stood very still and gradually
they became First Man and First Woman,
and that is how they Crane people
became the Crane Clan of the Ojibwa.

RETOLD FROM THE OJIBWA

On the Firing Line

Other than hazardous power lines and stealthy Coyote predators, one potential problem faced by biologists of the Grays Lake/Bosque Whooping Crane project was Snow Geese hunting. Limited hunting seasons became prevalent for Sandhills in New Mexico in the 1980s and in some other states of the Rocky Mountain Corridor, as they are in all the states, with the exception of Nebraska, of the Aransas/Wood Buffalo migratory pathway of Whooping Cranes. But the Whooping Crane, still numbering in the hundreds, is heavily protected. The Sandhill, numbering in the thousands in some states, is considered fair game.

Robert Porter Allen faced this problem, and, through cooperation with Canadian Fred Bard in Saskatchewan, the two acted as we have seen by putting out information and educating hunters up and down the flyway. At least, Allen and Bard, in the 1950s and 1960s, did not have to deal with the problem of Whoopers flying with flocks of Sandhills. Young Whoopers with their cinnamon-rusty feathers just going white in the first year look to an unpracticed eye like the gray-brown Sandhills.

Even the keen and practiced eye of the great avian artist John James Audubon did not distinguish Sandhills from Whoopers, labeling his Sandhill as a young Whooping Crane and defining the two quite different species as one species.

As America's most famous and most skilled bird artist, Audubon's gaffe is one that everyone who writes about birds — even to this day — takes aim at him in their pages. Furthermore, it is known that Audubon compounded his error when he took his rival artist, the canny Scot Alexander Wilson, to see Whooping Cranes in Kentucky. Consequently, Wilson too extended Audubon's mistake in his own work *Birds of the United States*, 1831. However, in later editions of

Sandhill Crane by John James Audubon—
(Audubon was in error when entitling this image "Whooping Crane, Young," possibly because young Whoopers are brownish in color).

Wilson's book, his editor Lucien Bonaparte saved Wilson from the legendary excoriations Audubon has received. Bonaparte corrected the error.

Hopefully, Audubon's error will be put to rest — at least in these pages, and we allow Audubon the latitude he deserves for his major work in depicting the Birds of America, so many species elegantly portrayed so accurately, including *Grus americana*, the adult Whooping Crane.

The young Whooper, Miracles, it seems, ended his first migration with his parents forty miles short of Bosque del Apache NWR. At the Bernardo State Waterfowl Management Area, Sandhills and Whoopers are protected, hunting controlled even to the point of sounding a siren when a flock of Sandhills lands accompanied by a young Whooping Crane. All hunting ceases at once.

Thus, Miracles and his Sandhill parents flew into Bernardo, a Waterfowl Management Area run by the State of New Mexico, and where hunting is permissible in parts of the area at the time he was there. Miracles had to pass over a "legal firing line every day" to get to his parents' feeding area. His adroitness at escaping the hunters' blasting was in a great part due to the wary teaching of his foster parents.

However, one hunter was apprehended who "claimed that Sandhill Cranes were 'large grey ducks.'" Therefore, a careless hunter gives the true hunter a bad name, and the voices of the people who care about birds sing out in rage against all hunters.

But just as there are those at the wheel of a two- or ten-ton vehicle, some skilled drivers, some half-asleep or drugged out, or novice drivers, there are shoddy hunters and there are skilled hunters who know everything there is available to know about the birds they hunt.

One of the skilled hunters I have in mind hunts Sandhills in West Texas where they also flock in great numbers. And he hunts them under legal conditions.

"Tiny," a U.S. Army retired colonel, goes every year with a group of fellow hunters and a guide to hunt Sandhill Cranes. Called "Tiny" because he stands well over six feet, he truly knows the bird he hunts. Nebraska born, when he talks of Sandhills, his eyes take on a special look. That special look has a great deal of know-how and a clear devotion to wildlife behind it.

Tiny spends only a few short weeks hunting in the field compared to the endless hours he devotes to wildlife conservation the rest of the year. His most recent project — and admittedly one dear to my heart — is to raise funds for the Trumpeter Swan restoration. One in which

Ruth Shea, married to Rod Drewien, is as valiant in the Swan's survival as Drewien is the Crane's.

This is not his only project. Tiny is not only one of the officers of Natureworks, an organization dedicated to wildlife conservation and wildlife art, but he is also a staunch supporter of Ducks Unlimited, an organization of hunters which has long toiled to save the wetland for waterfowl and waterbirds such as Swans or Cranes, and which has done so since the 1930s — long before the crisis in the disappearance of wetland habitat was even recognized by most.

There are many current horror stories which a game manager may tell you. There are those people — I won't dignify them with the honorific "sport hunter" — who shoot illegally from cars into woodlands at deer, or take out their frustrations at not finding game by punctuating with shot the silhouetted image of a deer on signs marking a deer crossing. But the worst evidence I have seen is on the narrow twisting roads through ranchland in that immense region of Osage County in Oklahoma not too far from where the Nature Conservancy has restored the Tallgrass Prairie and returned the Bison to it.

One late fall day in the mid-1990s while searching for wild migrating Trumpeter Swans from Minnesota and Wisconsin, I drove along a county road littered with so many bloody remains that not even the Crows deigned to alight and peck at them. All were headless raw carcasses of deer.

It seemed those engaged in the pursuit were not hunters such as Tiny; they were those who only shot deer for the trophy antlers.

Not only are modern game management stories replete with malefic tales of human to animal, but Native American mythologies and legends have many tales running through them of the "evil hunter." Probably the most well-known is the Ojibwa story collected by Henry Rowe Schoolcraft and put into poetry by Henry Wadsworth Longfellow. It tells of three brothers, two are honorable, but one is dishonorable. First, he breaks his word not to kill any animal, except those agreed upon. Not only does the wrongful brother break his word to his brothers, but he also attempts to kill the Red Swan with magic arrows he

German woodcut, by DAVID HOOGSTRATEN, *1701*, illustrating the Aesop Fable of "The Fox and the Crane."

yellow crane pavilion:
from ts'ui hao

the yellow crane
comes & carries
him off to live forever

they build a pavilion
to mark the spot

the yellow crane
never comes back

white clouds, millennia,
long, empty, long, slow

clear river light on each
bright han-yang leaf

lush, lush grass
on parrot island

sun goes down

where is home now?

mist over water moving

it makes a person think

ANSELM HOLLO

steals from their dead father's medicine bag, and which he is forbidden to touch. After a barrage of arrows let loose from his bow, he pierces the neck of the Red Swan with an arrow, but the swan magically arises from the water and flies off toward the setting sun, in Longfellow's words: "reddening the waters with its blood" (*Hiawatha*).

Like the true hunter who follows in the steps of the animal he hunts and also reveres, Aldo Leopold, of "land ethic" fame, himself once a hunter, and then a Wildlife Manager in the early days of the 1930s, a time when managing wildlife was coming into its own, pondered the paradoxical ways of some hunters, whom he obviously knew. Leopold came up with several questions and one succinct answer to them that any honorable hunter might follow, and some indeed do:

"Few sportsmen have ever tried the sport of learning something about the game they pursue, the wildlife they see, or the plants they tramp over. Why is this species here? Whence does it come, where go? What are its prospects of survival? What peculiarities of habit and habitat comprise the standard of living? To always seek but never quite achieve a bag limit of answers to such questions is the sport of the future" (*Swans*).

Unfortunately, not all hunters (as we saw with the "Sandhills as gray ducks" remark and the deerslayers) are skilled and have the expertise of a Tiny. Thus, hunting in the wintering area of Cranes was a problem for Drewien. Needless to say, the Bosque Refuge staff continues to fine-tune and to manage the Snow Goose season, especially when the Cranes appear.

Miracles survived his first year to return to the area near Grays Lake and to migrate again and again. Fortunately, he wasn't the only Whooper Rod Drewien and his team had to track, for each year there were newly fledged Whoopers. But Miracles became a famous white bird with reports from every birder or farmer who saw him and recognized him. So his errant wanderings were reported and duly recorded in Drewien's log.

With five fledglings in its first year, the Grays Lake project had already surpassed the captive breeding of Crip and Josephine. With their production of over fifty eggs, only four hatchlings survived. Now with good production, the wild Grays Lake to Bosque Rocky Mountain Population appeared to be an established one.

By 1984/85, ten years after the program began, an estimated number of cross-fostered Whoopers on the wing rose to a "record high of thirty-seven Cranes." This then equalled the number of wild Aransas/ Wood Buffalo Population twenty years before. Furthermore, the four-

170

teen Whooper 1975 nests in Canada from which Kuyt took single eggs hatched out eight fledgling chicks.

By now Miracles and his Houdini-like extrications from assorted dangers — from careless hunters and stealthy four-footed predators — seemed to prove himself as a wild Crane. An escape artist of the first degree.

Consequently, Miracles was thought old enough and sufficiently mature to have a mate. Strangely enough, the Grays Lake foster-reared Cranes seemed to lean toward a predominance of males. And so "Too Nice," called so at Patuxent for her coy and submissive behavior where she was "parent-reared," came from Maryland to Idaho. She was put in an enclosure where Miracles would see her.

And Miracles was definitely interested. He flew, says Doughty quoting Drewien, "at least sixteen times back and forth" to where she was. Then, still on the wing, he would speed off and chase Sandhills from his chosen territory — a dominant trait he had displayed early on even though reared by Sandhills.

Whooper and offspring. Cranes do not nest until between 3-7 years old and then usually lay only two eggs each year. Sadly, only one chick generally survives, but Cranes may live for 25-30 years in the wild and the one chick raised each year will likely fledge and join the migratory flock. The survival strategy of Cranes depends on caring for each precious new Crane.

When reading Doughty's detailed chronicle of what happened with the rendezvous of Miracles and Too Nice, you realize again how incredibly fortunate, first Pete and Josephine's pairing to produce eggs, then Josephine's mating with Crip to produce the young chick Rusty was. For ultimately things did not go well in the Rocky Mountain mating.

Miracles it is true grew familiar with Too Nice's presence in his territory, and she was released to wander freely, reverting to her wild self. But Miracles seemed to wax more aggressive toward the Sandhills, and, rather than pairing with his lady, he spent his time chasing and clearing the area of other Crane intrusions. Ever the jealous guardian.

Too Nice survived five months, some of the time hiding out in the freedom of the marsh or wandering with the Sandhills or other Whoopers. Past the time for breeding season, she was shipped back to Patuxent to winter there.

Again that next spring, Too Nice, sufficiently mature to mate, was sent back to Grays Lake where Miracles returned again safely from migration. Happily, Miracles appeared to take an even deeper interest in

Grus, *indeed is a*
very ancient form,
its remains appearing
in the Miocene of
France and Greece,
as well as in the
Pliocene and
Post-pliocene of
North America.
In France too, during
the "Reindeer Period"
there existed a
huge species—the
Grus primigenia
of M. Alphonse
Milne-Edwards—
which has doubtless
been long extinct.

PROFESSOR J. NEWTON
Encyclopedia Britannica,
1896

his proposed mate, showing signs of nesting by "piling bulrushes and cattails together" (Doughty).

Just on the verge of what could only look like a tendency towards successful bonding, a tragedy occurred only two days after Miracles showed inclinations to nest.

Ever the research scientist, Rod Drewien recorded the event in a photograph. It had to take enormous courage in that "decisive moment" when his camera clicked.

A first glance at the photo and you see only the enormous beauty of sky, mountain, and still marshy lake.

But in the foreground is the low-flying and miraculous white Crane dead — Miracles entangled on impact with a barbed wire fence. "The noblest flyer" — upside down now, his neck oddly bent snakes along the ground, the gallant wings loosely half unfurled as if to begin a threat display, and the great long black Whooping Crane leg held upright between the top two twisted wires, two more wires turned to catch the base of his long leg. Four wires in all, twisted into two.

The three toes, pied-de-grue, of the captured leg point skyward towards a blue spring, the center toe, its long nail curling into the sky seems to reach farther up than even the snowcapped peak of a far distant Idaho mountain.

First Light

Just after five A.M., the last darkness in the dry cold New Mexico air seems to be a chill falling to the coldest temperature possible on earth: absolute zero — minus 459.4 F.— the temperature near which are kept the entrails in the receivers of the Very Large Array.

Beneath the Bosque Refuge sight-deck, water is motionless. My toes, inside two pairs of socks and rough-out thick-soled hiking boots, feel too numb to ever be warm again.

The barrel of my long-range lens is cold even through my gloves, the camera loaded with ultra high-speed film to record the moment of first light. The other Audubon Society members are at the ready too, with cameras on tripods and spotting scopes all put deftly and silently in place.

In the last moonlight, the silver platter of the marsh is still. To our left, thousands of slumbering Snow Geese ride gently; their dark shapes, surrounded by silver eddies, are barely visible against the water.

Far out on the horizon of the lake a great string of roosting Sandhills sleep in single file line, dark beads on a long string.

A yellow streak along the eastern horizon, and the dark sinuous outline of the gentle mountain peaks comes into focus behind the Cranes.

The glow grows more intense, turns to rose, announcing the sun's warmth returning.

And then near us, a sound like no other sound on the planet: forty thousand wings beat upward; a million pinion feathers whistle and click in the dawn quiet. One holy rushing roar, and the Snow Geese ascend into the sky, breaking into scattered orderly squadrons, they speed toward the feeding grounds,

Firstlight with Snow Geese and Cranes, Bosque del Apache, New Mexico.

their white shapes, apparent at last, flaking against the background of a blue-gray mountain.

As the sun begins to make its presence felt, I see far out, one solitary long neck untie from the recesses of a wing. Among the roosting Sandhills, one sentinel Crane is awake.

Another head and neck comes up, the gray-brown bodies still dark beads. But one after one, the Sandhills' heads and necks appear. The sun rises, a great red semi-circle casting long arms of orange and pink light across the yielding darkness of the sky.

Much head turning and bobbing as the Sandhills converse, exchange greetings, leaping upward, even doing a little of their pair-bonding dance. Then one by one they follow the sentinel Crane, and they open their great wings to lift them aloft in the clear dawn air of a New Mexico winter sky.

Sandhill Crane in flight.

*A Special Cadre
of Crane Voyagers*

There were great numbers of waterfowl,

wading in the shoal water that covers

the sandy points to a vast distance

from the shores: they were geese,

brant and the beautiful

whooping crane.

WILLIAM BARTRAM
*Travels through North and South Carolina,
Georgia, East and West Florida, 1791*

South to Florida

If you happened by chance to sit next to Marianne Wellington on a plane, snapping on your seat-belt, getting ready for take-off, and wondering if that great metallic winged body of the jet will ascend into the sky where no one belongs except the birds, you might happen to strike up a conversation with the young traveler beside you.

If you're at all curious about your seatmate, you could try a little "social geography;" that is, you might attempt to locate her within the context of where she's from and who she is — a ploy of most travellers whenever faced with a few (hopefully) dull hours aloft rooted to the confines of an airline seat. And, since you're travelling from Milwaukee, you might first ask her if she's from Wisconsin.

She will no doubt answer in the affirmative and if she elaborates on where she lives in Wisconsin, you might be able to guess, from her obvious poise and diction, that she's some sort of junior executive, a teacher or a scientist. But unless she tells you precisely what she does — and she might — you will probably never guess her occupation. Her answer to the three lines of endeavor you guessed could all be "Yes."

For Marianne Wellington is a biologist, an executive, and a teacher. Yet she has one of those rarest of teaching jobs in the world, and, in performing her work, she wears a long white costume, a double face mask, and, on one hand, she sports a puppet.

No, she's not teaching young school children to perform, she's teaching young Whooping Cranes to fly and to survive in the wild in such places as Florida's Kissimmee Prairie. She's a Field Biologist, the Crane's surrogate mother, and the Assistant Cu-

Detail of a map by William Bartram showing a Crane and palm tree in foreground and Cranes dancing in a distant wetland (*original at the American Philosophical Society, Philadelphia*).

rator of Birds at International Crane Foundation in Baraboo, Wisconsin. To use E.O. Wilson's words about another field biologist, Marianne Wellington is a "born naturalist" and a member of a "special cadre of field biologists."

Just back from China to study the welfare of Black-necked Cranes, Jim Harris, Deputy Director (now President) of ICF, describes a rare moment in a Wisconsin field with Marianne and fledgling chicks:

"I will never forget those evenings. Marianne and I looked most strange in flowing white sheets, white sleeves, and a white puppet-glove with black moustache on one hand to serve as a bird head. The cool air over the prairie excited the chicks. At first they followed us, thin legs striding through the grass, but soon they swept those black-tipped wide wings to full length and took-off in great swift circles…. I stood motionless, my eyes raised skywards. The wild, so rare cranes circled faster than my neck could turn. Yet despite all their freedom, they hastened back, wings beating feathers rustling to drop so close beside me on the ground and rejoin the mother-father figures frozen with the moment." (*ICF Bugle*).

Jim Harris and Marianne Wellington are two of the Crane caregivers of the twenty-seven or so staff, counting everyone from interns to the Director George Archibald whom you might meet in spring, summer, or fall when the Crane Foundation welcomes the public. Even though the public visitors are not there in winter, the work with Cranes goes on. In late fall, each year since the early 1990s, Marianne Wellington goes to Florida to participate in the release of Whooping Crane in the wilds of the Kissimmee Prairie region. She is there with ICF's Whooping Crane contribution — along with Patuxent's — to the feral flock established in Florida in 1993. Six years after their release, the Florida Whoopers number close to seventy.

Florida was named *Pascua Florida*, "Easter feast day of Flowers," in 1513 by Ponce de Leon searching for the fountain of youth. Among other many natural wonders such as the unique ecozone the Everglades, Florida is an ancient Whooping Crane home and the present traditional home of a resident flock of Florida Sandhills and wintering Greater Sandhills (mentioned earlier).

That the Whooping Cranes were assuredly there in Florida once is undergirded by Alexander Sprunt, Jr.'s work *Florida Birdlife* published in 1954, the year Aransas /Wood Buffalo Whooper's nesting area was found in Canada. Sprunt, basing his work upon Arthur Howell's earlier

Florida Sandhill
Grus canadensis pratensis

Florida Birdlife published in 1932, speaks of "definite evidence of the occurrence of this species (*Grus americana*) in the state is furnished by the finding of its bones in Pleistocene deposits at Melbourne, Seminole and on the Itchuknee River."

For hundreds of years, the Whooper had not been seen in Florida, but many Floridians thought they were still there. Sprunt remarks that "there are those in Florida who will always ridicule the idea that the Whooping Crane does not occur now [in 1954]. For the simple reason that the Florida Sandhill Crane is invariably known throughout the state as a "Whooping Crane." Such a bird [as the Whooper], even larger than the crane they know, snow-white in plumage with black tipped wings [if it did appear] might well be considered a composite ghost of all cranes they ever knew."

In 1993, the Whooping Crane did appear in Florida. The establishment of a flock by releasing birds from ICF and Patuxent is part of an overall plan of the Whooping Crane Recovery Team. The "long-term objective of the plan is to create (in addition to the Aransas/Wood Buffalo Cranes) two more self-sustaining populations." Then, the Recovery Team hopes to eventually remove the Whooper from the Endangered List and "down-list its status to threatened" (Meine and Archibald).

The Grays Lake to Bosque Whooping Cranes (Rocky Mountain Population) was part of that plan. However, in 1986, scientists decided that the cross-fostering of Sandhill parent rearing Whooping Cranes caused "mal-imprinting." To their horror one of the Sandhills mated with a Whooper and produced a hybrid "Whoophill".

Fortunately, "only one interspecific pair formed, and only one Whoophill was produced. Furthermore, "the Sandhills were not imprinted on the Whooper Cranes, and they most likely rejected the advance of the Whooping Cranes. Within any population we have a level of variation that apparently allowed one Sandhill to pair with a Whooper." (Archibald, personal communication).

After considerable study of several other sites, the team chose Florida for the "new" or reintroduced flock. Stephen Nesbitt (whom you met earlier measuring Sandhill beaks for gender) of Florida Fish and Game was to oversee it. Because the Whoopers would not have parents to teach

Typically, Cranes run into the wind to achieve the lift they need for flight, but if startled a Crane can immediately begin to fly.

them to migrate, their flock would be non-migratory and, therefore, year-round residents of Florida like their "shirt-tail" relatives the Florida Sandhills.

There are not only the Whooping Crane's ancient bones to prove their early presence in Florida, but there are also observations by naturalists from as early as the seventeenth century. William Hilton, in his 1644 document relating a "Discovery Lately Made on the Coast of Florida," writes of an Indian telling him of great quantities of "swans, geese and cranes" in wintertime (Rogers and Hammer).

By the 1700s there were reliable reports to prove that there were indeed Florida wintering Whoopers. The proof that they were white Cranes as well as gray-brown Sandhills is the kind of hard evidence that even Robert Porter Allen would accept in his research into the early whereabouts of the Whooper. The proof led him to assert with confidence that the Whooper one hundred and fifty years ago flew as "migrants across the Appalachians from wintering grounds on the Atlantic seaboard"(TWCRR).

The Hooping Crane

In the year of our Lord, 1722, Mark Catesby, a gentleman of quality, set sail for the new world in the month of February. He arrived in Charleston, then Charles Town, on May 3 of that same year. By June 22, he had already made a trip "40 miles up the country."

Catesby's purpose in undergoing this long voyage for the second time was to collect seeds and specimens of plants to send back to England. But he became so fascinated with the animals, particularly the birds of the country, that his original mission enlarged and extended to documenting not only the plants but also the New World animals. Thus, Catesby created an encompassing natural history of the southern Atlantic coast. He describe the bird species, and he learned to depict them, creating a work which is nothing short of phenomenal.

Catesby's great work, *The Natural History of Carolina, Florida and the Bahama Islands*, which I have had the good fortune to hold in my hands — wearing white gloves, of course, at Gilcrease Art Museum — was published in 1774 in English and French. An immense undertaking: Catesby (pronounced cat's-bee) had to teach himself to draw the birds in order to depict them and then went on to execute the hand-colored

Considered the first drawing of a Whooping Crane by a European— Mark Catesby. *(collection of Gilcrease Museum)*

engravings. He delineated, with both images and words, one hundred and nine species—seventy-five of which are the sources for their taxonomic classifications under the hands of his great contemporary Carolus Linnaeus. Furthermore, he depicted three more species from the Bahamas, making a grand total of seventy-eight species. Today, a biologist who discovers a new species and puts a descriptive name to it has the kind of immortal place in history which Joseph Kastner calls the

16th century woodcut by CONRAD GESNER of a Eurasian Crane, *Grus grus.*

Also known as the Common Crane, it is the third most numerous Crane after the Sandhill and Demoiselle. The most widely distributed of Cranes, they can be found in over 85 Eurasian and African countries! Well-protected and well-loved in Scandinavian countries, their return is celebrated as a sign of spring to residents tired of winter. Cranes stage at Hornborga, Sweden, and often over a 100,000 people from all parts of Europe come to enjoy their appearance.

"species of eternity." However, only the great Bull-frog, *Rana catesbiana,* gives Catesby his own ticket to eternal fame.

Unlike John James Audubon who a century later worked primarily with dead birds which he shot and brought home to arrange in life-like poses, Catesby worked in the field drawing the living birds: "The animals, particularly the Birds I painted while alive (except a very few) and gave them their Gestures peculiar to every kind of Bird, and where it could be admitted, I have adapted the Birds to those Plants on which they fed, or have relation to."

One exception to the live birds Catesby drew is an important one. For Catesby, as far as is believed, is absolutely the first European to clearly depict a Whooping Crane, and he has made a verbal description which for so early a time is astounding and follows the procedure of most Europeans of comparing the "new" animals — new to the Europeans — which they see to the ones back home. Thus he uses the term "Common Crane," once common to England but now uncommon. It is currently called the Eurasian Crane (*Grus grus*):

"It is about the size of the Common Crane. The bill is brown and six inches long; the Edges of both mandibles, towards the End about an Inch and half are serrated. A deep and broad channel runs from the Head more than half way along its upper Mandible. Its Nostrils are very large. A broad white List runs from the eye obliquely to the Neck except which the Head is brown. The Crown of the Head is callous and very hard thinly beset with stiff black hairs which lie flat, and are so thin that the Skin appears bare of a reddish Flesh-color. Behind the Head is a Peak of black feathers. The large wing feathers are black. All the rest of the Body is white."

Catesby ends by telling how he took these descriptions from the "entire skin of the Bird" which was presented to him by an "Indian who made use of it for his Tobacco-pouch." Furthermore the Indian told Catesby that in early spring "Great multitudes" of them "frequent the lower Parts of the Rivers near the Sea; and then return to the Mountains in the Summer." Insecure with just one source, Catesby double-checked on the Crane's whereabouts with another man who confirmed that the Crane's make a "remarkable noise—and that he had seen them at the mouth of the Savannah, Aratemaha and other Rivers near St. Augustine [Florida]," but that he had never "seen any as far north as the Carolinas."

Clearly, because Catesby had only the Whooper's skin, he had never heard them, but he called them "Hooping Crane" as did other Europeans apparently for the Hoop! Hoop! shouting of English hunters.

Age of Reason

By Catesby's time, the eighteenth century, a great schism began to be felt as Science and the Humanities parted ways. The Humanities is a term arising in the Renaissance to denote the scholarly studies of the newly recovered texts of Greek and Latin, but the term has enlarged through time to include scholarly studies which are not science. Thus Humanities refers to and includes Theology, Philosophy, and the Arts. The rift between science and the humanities became so marked that by the twentieth century, English writer C.P. Snow spoke of the two as "two separate cultures."

No longer would Naturalists include the folklore and myth or the symbolism which hovered around animals and plants. Those cultural connotations which shape human perception of animals are sometimes for the good, sometimes for the bad. For example, because the eagle has never been domesticated, its mighty and powerful image seems wildly appropriate on U.S. coins and bills. On the other hand, probably because it has been domesticated, the Turkey—Benjamin Franklin's suggestion for our national symbol — is looked upon as humorous even though wild Turkeys may give a modern-day hunter a hard day's merry chase in the field. The Turkey (*Meleagris gallopavo*) is indeed endemic to the U.S. and clearly native to North America. Catesby was imbued with the caveats of English naturalist John Ray who exhorted Naturalists against any descrip-

Crane amongst exaggerated flowers of Florida, detail of a William Bartram drawing *(original in the Natural History Museum, London)*.

tions of the biotic world which would include "morals, fables, presages." Even though their inclusion had long been the case. But by the eighteenth century, Naturalists were to base their taxonomic descriptions on observation. Information was to be gleaned by "observation alone."

In the eighteenth century, scientific thought was dominated by the discoveries of Isaac Newton. Thus, the pure laws of Physics ruled, and the age of pure science was born. Scientists worked with what they considered to be value-free attitudes, each one a removed and objective observer of the natural world, a condition in startling contrast to the values of theologians, philosophers and artists.

The Naturalists' long affinity especially with the arts was overwhelmed by the pure white immaculate reason of physics and mathematics. If Biology had been the dominant science of the last three hundred years we would have very different cultural views. But with the laws of Newton's physics, the world and indeed the universe was looked upon as a machine. Nature which supposedly chugged along was separate and apart from humans. It was out there — outside the factory, the house, the office building.

This three-hundred year era is what Philosopher Ken Wilbur calls "Modernity," a term which encompasses the basic differentiation of Science vis-a-vis theology, philosophy (Wilbur uses the term "morals" to include both) and the arts. This splitting apart of what

Detail of map of Alachua Savanah by William Bartram showing Cranes flying over Florida wetlands *(original at the American Philosophical Museum, Philadelphia).*

Snow called "cultures" into the value-free (science) and the value-laden (morals/art) led to the problems many scholars see with us today in modern life: the fragmentation and disassociation of the individual, the loss of the spiritual, and the great separation from the natural world.

However, Wilbur points out that the splitting of the two cultures did have positive aspects in opening the way for such great movements as our democracy and freedom of the individual, and, furthermore, scholars in science, theology, philosophy, and the arts were free to pursue their way without the encumbrance of the other.

Many, like Wilbur the philosopher, have considered this modern problem of fragmentation and have sought in their own way to point towards a new kind of unity in the belief that what Thomas Kuhn calls a "paradigm shift" is occurring. In other words, a vast and drastic transition from old models of thought to totally new ways of perceiving the world is coming about with the new millennium in a period some call "post-modern."

Willis Harman, social scientist, thinker and scholar, sees the transition as a "global mind change" and a "promise in the twenty-first century."

"We are living," says Harman, "through one of the most fundamental shifts in history — a change in the actual belief structure of Western society."

Furthermore, Harman believes that "there is no conflict between the 'perennial wisdom' of the world's spiritual tradtions and a science based on M-3 [metaphysical, or inclusion of the spiritual] assumptions" (*Mind Change*).

Another thinker and a visionary scientist Fritjof Capra defines the change as a "definite movement towards wholeness, toward a dynamic view, toward a participatory universe where you don't separate the observed from the observer, and these various characteristics are expressed in science and in society" (*Thinking*).

One of the most articulate and visible scientists thinking upon these problems is naturalist Edward O. Wilson. In his work *Consilience: the Unity of Knowledge*, Wilson uses the word consilience" as it was used by William Whewell in his 1840 synthesis *The Philosophy of Inductive Sciences*. Thus Wilson means consilience to be "literally a jumping together of knowledge by the linking of facts and fact-based theory across disciplines to create a common ground-work."

Wilson believes that "if the world really works in a way so as to encourage the consilience of knowledge ... the enterprises of culture will eventually fall into science [that is, natural science] and the humanities, particularly the creative arts."

Through all these scholars' words appears a common theme which animal behaviorist Jane Goddall puts most succinctly. For she believes through each individual's actions to improve the world, we have *Reason for Hope*.

Mark Catesby, unhampered by cultural notions of plants and animals, went on with great care to delineate the Whooping Crane both verbally and visually even though his portrait of the Whooper is just that: a portrait. Head and neck are clearly drawn. When Robert Porter Allen comes upon Catesby's work after researching everything he could

The birds were reflected in the clear marsh waters. . . . Magic birds were dancing in a mystic marsh. The grass swayed with them. The earth was dancing with the crane, and the low sun, and the wind and sky.

MARJORIE KINNAN RAWLINGS
The Yearling

William Bartram's
drawing of
Florida Sandhill
Grus canadensis pratensis
"Wattola Great
Savanah Crane"
*(original in the
British Museum).*

find from pre-Colonial and Colonial times he exclaims that it is not until Catesby "that we reach the end of this long span of ignorance regarding the identity and appearance of Grus americana."

Consequently, from Catesby's work, Allen was sure there were Whooping Cranes on the Atlantic Seaboard, and assuredly in Florida. Fifty years after Catesby, another naturalist made forays down the Atlantic into Florida. William Bartram, son of the great Quaker naturalist John Bartram, holds the distinction of being the first American-born naturalist of European stock.

William Bartram made his way to the Carolinas, Georgia and Florida. He had traveled before with his father, and young Bartram's later work, *Travels through North and South Carolina, Georgia and East and West Florida* in 1791, abounds not only with botanical lore for which he was most famous but also with vivid Crane descriptions. William Bartram, unlike Catesby who did not always recognize the tribal differences, knew the native tribes and spoke of how one Indian Nation differed from the other. His many maps, drawn as if from a Crane's eye view, include Indian dwellings as well as the animals and plants. Frequently Cranes hover in the air above the Florida landscape.

In Bartram's list of the myriad birds he witnessed in their native habitat, he give a clear description of both the Whooping Crane (which he called *Grus clamator*) and the Sandhill, the resident of Florida, which he called by the name it still has *Grus canadensis pratensis* — the Savannah Crane. On his depiction of the Sandhill, Bartram labeled it with a native word "Wattola."

Traveling over four years as he did, Bartram of course had to subsist on the land. He had to eat whatever the hunters accompanying him on his travels took.

Consequently, though he did have to eat the Sandhill, and his remark that "Sandhills make good soup" has been often quoted, he goes on to say: "Nevertheless, as long as I can get any other necessary food, I shall prefer his seraphic music in the ethereal skies, and my eyes and understanding gratified in observing the economy and social communities in the green savannahs of Florida."

Bartram's description of the Florida Sandhill was useful to European scientists such as George Edwards who pondered the New World animals. Bartram's descriptions reverberate with the travelling naturalist's great passion for the world of plant and animal:

"This stately bird is above six feet in length from the extremity of the beak when extended, and the wings expand eight or nine feet; they are above five feet when standing erect; the tail is remarkably short, but the flag or pendant feathers which fall down the rump on each side, are very long and sharp pointed, of a delicate texture, and silky softness; the beak is very long, strait, sharp-pointed; the crown of the head bare of feathers, of a reddish rose color, thinly barbed with short, stiff, black hair; the legs and thighs are very long, and bare of feathers a great space above the knees; the plumage of this bird is generally of a pale ash color with shade or clouds of pale brown and sky blue, the brown prevails on the shoulders and back, the barrels of the quill-feathers are long and of a large diameter, leaving a large cavity when extracted from the wing; all the bones of this bird have a thin shell and consequently a large cavity or medullary receptacle. When these birds move their wings in flight, their strokes are slow, moderate and regular, their shafts and webs upon one another, creak as the joints of working of a vessel in a tempestuous sea" (*Travels*).

Before Bartram, Mark Catesby had suggested something of the possibilities of migrations; in fact, he later presented a paper to the Royal Society to prove that Swallows did not go underground in winter and hibernate — as was believed at the time. But Bartram's discourse on migration was invaluable information to George Edwards; his educated guess was that there were at least two flyways in North America, and he is the first to come up with this idea.

18th century drawing of a Whooping Crane, *Grus americana,* (note how the Crane is standing on a larger version of its head) by GEORGE EDWARDS, *1693-1773,* a British naturalist whose descriptions of twenty-three birds were contributed by William Bartram *(Oxley Nature Center).*

Among many extensive facts of migration, Bartram writes: "very few tribes of birds build or rear their young in the south or maritime part of Virginia, and Carolina, Georgia and Florida; yet all these numerous tribes, particularly the soft-billed kinds, which breed in Pennsylvania, passing the spring season through the region in a few weeks time...."
Thus William Bartram, like Mark Catesby before him, created new pathways for the burgeoning science of Biology to follow — even though

White-Naped Crane
Grus vipio
19th century engraving

White-naped Cranes breed in eastern Russia and China and winter in the Koreas, southern Japan, and east central China. They are the fourth rarest Crane, although numbers have increased to about 5,000. Wetland destruction from agricultural expansion threatens the habitat of these birds.

neither Biology nor Ornithology as sciences had yet become formal disciplines. For, as Paul Lawrence Farber says in his *Discovering Birds: The Emergence of Ornithology as a Scientific Discipline, 1760-1850:* "the word Biology came into use in the early 1800s to describe what was then perceived to be a new study of the living world." And, according to Farber, the study of Ornithology as a formal science was shaped by two major works which were new types of bird studies in their precise organization of data. Their authors, both French and in the vanguard of the new science, are Mathurin-Jacques Brisson (1723-1806) *Ornithologie* and George-Louis Leclerc de Buffon (1707-1888) *Histoire Naturelle des Oiseaux,* the "natural history of birds." The period in which these two scientists wrote their multi-volumed works is the period of "new data," 1770-1830, when so much information poured in to Europe from all over the world, that, even without computers, it too could be called the Information Age.

First Americans

In the 1700s, when naturalists such as Catesby and Bartram traveled the southeast, Bartram going south from the Carolinas into Georgia, Florida and Alabama, they encountered many of the original tribal people living there. And the naturalist's point of view towards the first inhabitants of the New World differed greatly from settlers, soldiers, or missionaries. The settlers were there for land; the soldiers to protect them in its acquisition; the missionaries to harvest souls. But the early naturalists, not seeking territory in the form of land or spirit, but seeking knowledge of the biota, shared the veneration for the plants and animals which Native Americans held.

William Bartram particularly honored the people whom he met on his four-year journey, principally the Cherokee, Chickasaw, Choctaw, Creek and Seminole tribes which Europeans called the Five Civilized Tribes. A century later the people were forced from their rich lands in a most uncivilized fashion beginning in 1836 with the "Great Removal."

Whooping Crane poised to lunge its beak "down like a spear."

By government decree, the tribes were forced to give up their land and walk over what the Cherokee call the Trail of Tears to Indian Territory, now Oklahoma, far to the west of them.

One tribe, the Calusa, vanished as a tribe during the Great Removal, preferring to join the Seminole who escaped Removal by disappearing into the Everglades. But the Calusa left behind many names in their Muskogean language for rivers, savannahs, and swamps, calling the Kissimmee River the "long flowing water."

Another tribe, the Creek, also Muskogean language speakers, Bartram found to be quite striking in appearance: "tall, erect, with an open countenance, dignified and placid, yet the forehead and

high tide at Shiogoshi
crane leg splashed
sea-cool

BASHO
1644-94

brow formed, as to strike you instantly with heroism and bravery." The Creeks have a story told by a modern Muskogee-Creek storyteller, which contains ancient truths of their reverence for the animals, particularly the white Crane:

"In the beginning all the animals were just one color. The Great One, the Master of Breath, told the First Child that he could pick one of the animals to show him how to find the plants which would heal him whenever he was sick.

"First Child looked around and all the animals were hurrying towards him wearing new colors. The Blue Jay found some berries to turn its feathers blue. The Raccoon found some dark clay to put around its eyes, on its nose and tail. The Snake rubbed itself on some leaves and turned green. Every animal now wore new colors, so all the animals gathered in a circle to wait for First Child to choose from one of them.

"But one animal spent all its time busy catching fish, so it didn't have new color. First Child looked over all the animals' heads at the tall bird still all white with black-tipped wings, and First Child said, 'This Crane is so wise and it catches fish so easily that I choose it to instruct the tribe in the ways of healing the sick. It will be the Crane who will show our people where the healing herbs are to be found.'"

The Vanished White Crane Appears

On January 10, 1993, the first Whooping Cranes to return to their long-ago habitat arrived in Florida. These "Majestic" birds as Marty Folk, one of the Florida biologists, says of them were released into the wilds of central Florida savannahs, on a chain of ranchland in the Kissimmee Prairie area.

Like Canus the Whooper which was flown from Patuxent to Monte Vista, these young Whoopers did not arrive on their own. They were shipped very carefully from Patuxent Wildlife Research Center and the International Crane Foundation.

By 1999, the Florida Whooping Cranes showed evidence that they might be able to survive in the wild: they nested. In the spring of 2000, they began the 21st century by succeeding in hatching a pair of chicks. Thus, scientists had new hope for the Whooping Crane: the first pair, the male from Patuxent and the female from ICF, to produce their own young in the wild of the lower forty-eight states since Rusty emerged from the egg at Aransas Refuge in Texas under the startled and watchful eyes of Robert Porter Allen and his USFWS colleagues.

Stephen Nesbitt and Marty Folk, overseeing the Florida Cranes' welfare say -- "this historic pair of Whoopers showed us that Whooping Cranes raised in captivity can do what has to be done for the project to work -- reproduce themselves." (*Unison Call*).

Young Whooper.

Technologies and a Higher Power

On October 3, 2000, when thirteen imprinted Sandhill Cranes lifted off from Necedah Wildlife Refuge in Wisconsin on their way to winter in Florida, clearly they and the Operation Migration ultralight pilots leading them were not only drawing on a higher power but they were assisted as well by extraordinary technologies. The ultralight planes (Trikes) were equipped with Global Positioning Systems for tracking their whereabouts. Furthermore, the ultralights had digital sound equipment, vocalizers, programmed with Crane-calls telling the Cranes to "follow" or to "land".

For pilot/plane/crane to accomplish the nearly impossible flying trek southward over 3000 miles to Florida, stopping off on twenty-four overnights, took a special nudge from Elsewhere.

Although several were lost en route, the Cranes were truly blessed—as are we to still have them on this planet. Not only was their survival bolstered by a special cadre of veterinarians and avian biologists following on the ground during their extraordinary airborne excursion from Wisconsin to Florida's Chassahowitzka Wildlife Refuge, but also they were—and are—survivors of an environment radically altered by our own technologies, exponentially so from the beginning of the twentieth Century when the Wright Brothers first lifted off in 1903, and humans could go in their machines where the birds go.

The mere fact that Cranes are with us in the 21st century is an absolute miracle. When these "birds of peace" arrived in Florida, November 11, the holiday marked by the return of peace after war called "Veterans Day," they were met on the ground by puppet-gloved and white-gowned Crane biologists. Shortly after their arrival the Cranes would answer one of the questions scientists had asked themselves. When the ultralights rose aloft in a final farewell to their fellow travelers, scientists wondered if the Cranes would stay put at their destination and not follow as they had followed on the long southward journey.

Dancing Crane
from a Greek vase
"Duel of Heroes"—
Tiryns, 700 B.C.

But, eyeing the familiar gowned figures of the crane-like human scientists who had reared them, the Sandhills turned,and,quietly feeding,they stayed on at Chassahowitzka Wildlife Refuge. The Sandhills,like others of their species used in the cross-fostering experiment at Grays Lake, Idaho are the first to fly this particular Wisconsin/Florida route. In 2001, the plan is for Whoopers to follow the flight pattern south and thus begin the reign of another self-sustaining flock— a migratory one like the traditional Texas/Canada flock— with all the freedom and majesty of airborne Whooping Cranes.

Pilot Joseph Duff leads Cranes down to Florida as part of Operation Migration. "Many believe the techniques developed by Operation Migration offer the only hope for re-establishing migratory flocks of several endangered species. The OM team acts as surrogate parents, helping the birds imprint on the aircraft and conditioning them to fly with it. Later, when the birds are mature, they are led south by the OM team on a pre-determined route to a safe wintering site."

Look the Crowned Crane is dancing!
Crowned Crane praise-singing woman
During the day, the shameless one weaves.
Astonishing
The beginning of beginning rhythm
is speech of the Crowned Crane
The Crowned Crane says, "I speak."
The word is beauty.

FROM A RITUAL OF THE BAMBARA TRIBE, AFRICA

Voice of the Crane

O men, we have been taught the language of birds
and all favors have been showered on us.

THE KORAN

Tarawkow. The Crane.

JOHN WHITE

Referred to as the "Sloane Crane," this depiction is probably the earliest protrayal
by a European. It is thought by Sir Hans Sloane to be derived from the original
colored drawing by John White of the Roanoke Colony expedition (1585-86).
It was in the White family's possession when acquired by Sloane in 1706.
(Collection of the British Museum)

A Fall Morning: On the Way to Wisconsin

The last Ice Age which finally retreated withdrawing from the upper Midwest was named for the state of Wisconsin. The river, flowing through Wisconsin near Baraboo where the International Crane Foundation is located, is "the gathering of the waters".

The colossal glacier of the Wisconsonian Ice Age left behind not only the Great Lakes to mark its presence there, but it left profound traces on the land as well, some of which may be apparent to the traveler. On my way to Baraboo, Wisconsin, I note those traces, looking through the windshield of a Mercury station wagon loaded with books, papers and one large dog.

Setting out from the eastern shore of Lake Michigan, I've dipped down into Indiana, skirting the lake. Once I turn south off I-94, leaving the way to Chicago, the tempo slows, and I feel inclined to obey the injunction once seen on Indiana license plates to "wander Indiana." Indianans have embellished their farm entrances with corn shocks and pumpkins to announce the coming of Halloween.

In the skies the migrating Sandhills starting southward announce the equinox. They have set out from their nesting areas in marshes and ponds of Wisconsin and Michigan to their staging area in Jasper-Pulaski State Wildlife Refuge not far from Valparaiso, from which the great Glacial Lake Chicago, once towering over that city, ends to the east in the Valparaiso moraine, the outer limits of the last glacial advance.

The Cranes passing overhead, Greater Sandhills mostly, are on course along their traditional flyway from the upper Midwest to the southeast Atlantic states. They were sighted at the other end of their migration in pre-colonial Virginia by John White, who became the Governor of Roanoke, the lost colony, and Grandfather of Virginia Dare, the first European child born in the North America.

Before he was appointed Governor of Roanoke, John White came first to America as an artist recording the native people, animals, and plants for the expedition sent out to the New World by Sir Walter Raleigh. Some scholars believe there is indirect evidence that John White was also present on the first voyage in 1584 to the coasts when, in July 1584, Captain Amadas and Captain Barlowe, landing on the Island of

Wokokon found "great numbers of Cranes for most part white, and they made a noise or clamour as if an army of men shouted together."

The report of the captains is considered to be one of the first reports of Whooping Cranes in the New World. And John White who returned in 1585 was possibly the first artist of European stock to depict the Crane visually, labeling it in English merely "Crane" and adding, like William Bartram, the native name, the Algonquin's "Tarakowa."

White's pale blue and white watercolor drawing is part of the Sloane Collection in the British Museum. Historian Thomas P. Harrison in his work on John White's birds labels the drawing "Sandhill Crane." But another historian, Paul Hulton, who also denotes the Crane as Sandhill, qualifies his label by adding that the depiction "does not show the expected red and brown of the Sandhill, thus the identity of its race is not possible." It is possible that White's drawing, highly stylized in the manner of birds on coats of arms, could be a Whooper.

I enter the gates of Jasper-Pulaski wandering through the park in and out of time zones—one part of Indiana is on Central Standard Time another on Eastern Standard Time, so it could be Four P.M. or it could be Three P.M. when I find the field where the Sandhills congregate. They pass directly overhead in great slanting tiers of Crane and then stack up like planes at Chicago's O'Hare Airport, circling for a landing. There are at least a thousand Cranes in the air and on the green swelling ground, and the sound of their call fills the Indiana afternoon. A little later in October their numbers will grow to an army of thousands of Sandhills.

The thousands of Cranes arriving here are survivors from a thinning population of the upper Midwest in the 1930s when the great Aldo Leopold moved into his famous "Chicken Shack" on the Wisconsin River. There

Aldo Leopold and his wife Estella with their good dog, Flick.

on weekends from the University of Wisconsin at Madison, he began to write *A Sand County Almanac*. The words he wrote there still echo over the land in the voice of the Sandhill Crane.

Planting trees and working with his wife and children to restore the worn-out sandy land he had acquired, Leopold put into action with his own hands the words he wrote of the need for an ethical and responsible human stewardship of the land. To Leopold the few Sandhill Cranes he saw were what biologists call a "species indicator," an avian fingerprint and an indication of the welfare of the landscape. Their thin numbers only glimpsed in the sky once or twice gave evidence of the degradation of the Depression Era land.

A great deal of the restoration of Cranes to the upper Midwest is due to Leopold's work as a catalyst and shaper of opinion, opinion resulting in wetland protection and restoration. "Today," says George Archibald, "the Sandhills number more than twelve thousand in Wisconsin and perhaps more than thirty thousand in the Midwest."

George Archibald of the International Crane Foundation encountered Leopold's work in his student days at Cornell. The lives and work of the three very different individuals — Leopold, Sauey and Archibald — would converge in the landscape of Wisconsin and extend worldwide in the great and inspired hope to conserve the Cranes.

Born in Nova Scotia, Archibald writes:

"Soon after beginning my graduate studies of cranes at Cornell University Laboratory of Ornithology in 1968, I read for the first time *A Sand County Almanac*. Aldo Leopold's moving description of sandhill cranes in his essay 'Marshland Elegy' gave expression to what I had felt ever since first meeting cranes in the muskeg wilds of Canada. Three years later, when Ron Sauey arrived at Cornell, I was amazed to discover that his parents' home near Baraboo, Wisconsin was only a few miles away from the Leopold's family's famous 'shack' beside the Wisconsin River — the place where Leopold drew inspiration for his *Almanac*. In 1973, the International Crane Foundation was founded on the Sauey farm, and the Leopold shack became my spiritual retreat *(Elegy)*."

After leaving Jasper-Pulaski, I drive northward, stopping by the road occasionally to take a photo of more Sandhills still arriving at the

Black-Necked Crane
Grus Nigricollis —
a rare breed found in Tibet, Mongolia, and China. The last of fifteen species to be classified due to their remoteness. Its population is estimated at around 5,600-6,000. To its credit, China has developed 8 nature refuges for protection of critical habitat for Black-necked Cranes. Unfortunately, channelization of rivers for flood control, diversion of water for irrigation, tree plantations, and degradation caused by heavy livestock grazing has led to the disappearance of many of the wetlands used by these birds.

Red-Crowned Crane
Grus japonensis,
the second rarest species
of Crane with a
total population of
1,700-2,000.

park. Finally, I connect with Highway 30 going west towards the Illinois state line. I've gone this way more than once. For at least two or more times, at the very same juncture where Highway 30 makes a profound right angle jog, I have looked up from grid-locked traffic below to see a small echelon of thirty or so Sandhills. Reminders of the natural world, they slant precisely on course south and east toward Jasper-Pulaski.

Finally in Illinois, I pass through suburbia's city after city, all sprawling outward from Chicago. Then I angle northward into what was once, with the exception of Iowa, the richest farmland in America. But if the city planners and builders had ever heard of Aldo Leopold's principle of land ethic, they have chosen to take the road "more traveled by." Not only in Illinois but throughout the U.S., new houses and houses a-building sprout from the rich soil. Freshly laid cement on roads and driveways and in foundations of houses all harden into concrete over the good earth.

Passing northward into Wisconsin on a "road less travelled," I see if not another story, at least a more peaceful and wooded landscape. "Dane County," a sign beside the road proclaims. The sign reminds me of one of Wisconsin's distinguished zoologists, Dr. Philo Romayne Hoy, who in 1845, made an intense study of the then "present status of twenty-six Wisconsin birds." In the course of his research, Hoy gathered a bird-specimen and had it mounted, as was the custom then. Several were the Whooping Crane, some of the last to fly Wisconsin's skies and probably nesting in southern Wisconsin. Hoy reported to the Wisconsin Natural History Society with his paper "Man's Influence on the Avifauna of Southeastern Wisconsin." Significantly, "man's influence" tripled in thirty years with the tripling of the state's population.

In 1854, William Dudley, reporting to the Philadelphia Academy of Natural Sciences, named a species of Crane *Grus hoyianus* in honor of Dr. Hoy. It was a "species of Crane found in Wisconsin, presumed new."

However, Robert Porter Allen, making his research into Whooping Crane distribution, surmised from Dudley's description of *Grus hoyianus* that it was an immature Whooping Crane "shot on the Sugar River in Dane County" *(TWCRR)*.

One specimen of *Grus americana* mounted by Hoy now stands in the Ron Sauey Memorial Library built at ICF to honor Ron Sauey co-founder of ICF who died January 7, 1987, suddenly and tragically at the age of thirty-eight.

Brolga's dancing fame and beauty
was renowned and many men wished
to take her as a wife. Amongst the suitors
was the evil magician, Nonega, but the
elders said they would never consent to
the marriage. Enraged, Nonega waited
until one day when he found Brolga
dancing by herself on an open plain
near the camp—"If I cannot have
you, no one shall!" he uttered,
calling up a whirlwind which
surrounded the dancing girl.
When the whirlwind moved on,
there was no sign of Brolga . . .
just a large, grey long-legged
dancing bird. From that time to
this, the Aborigines have called
that bird Brolga, the beautiful,
dancing crane of the floodplains
of Northern Australia.

Brolga Crane
Grus rubicunda

When I began research on this book in the mid 1990s, I visited the Sauey library and was permitted to roam though the marvelous research texts on Cranes gathered there. I was aware then of the Crane's endowment of spirit of long-life and a kind of immortality. For I sensed Sauey's gentle presence, not in the taxidermy Whoopers "ghostlike presence," but as a coherent and vital force of the truly passionate young ornithologist.

Nearing the town of Baraboo on the highway passing on a road between rock strewn cliffs of the Baraboo Range, I sense the quartz memory of an Ice Age Creature beneath the tilting rocks. But Baraboo, with a population of ten thousand or so is probably more famous to tourists for its place in the history of the "Greatest Show on Earth." Once the winter home of Ringling Brothers Circus, the downtown area boasts the Circus World Museum. It was one of the Museum's early managers, Chappie Fox who encouraged Ron Sauey to pursue ornithology. Still active, Fox serves ICF as an honorary board member.

Driving through tree-lined Baraboo, I arrive at a major intersection with a stoplight. If I choose to go left, I will eventually arrive at Devil's Lake, an Ice Age remnant, a wonder to be seen on the "Ice Age Trail" through Wisconsin. But today I go right, ascend the hill on the empty street past seemingly silent houses. Silent and empty but for the lavish decorations, Green and White booster signs of the Green Bay Packers game, which give evidence that the game is obviously in progress.

On County Road A, I'm soon out of the town and in open country marked by the Ice Age tilting Rhyolite Quartz, the furrowed rilles and slanting dells of the Wisconsonian Age. I've been over this road several times, but I never tire of this miraculous open country landscape created in my imagination some thirty years ago at my own first encounter of Aldo Leopold's "Sand County." Looking ahead toward the distant line of pine tree forest, I imagine any living pine tree could tell you of Leopold's legacy.

Topping another hill, I see a Raccoon, road-killed, a Crow pecking at its sparse remains. Avoiding it, I wonder if that little striped black and white body holds the genetic memory of the Raccoon which managed to kill a Whooping Crane named "Tex."

Unison Call

Tex in her life reappears in the early 1980s photo taken by George Archibald's wife Kyoko. She photographed the two of them mid-stride, the man Archibald and the Whooper Tex. They share a stroll across the Wisconsin field. George, bearded then, has his hands in the pockets of worn jeans. He strolls leisurely across the field, the outline of his body limned by the upright craning neck of the Whooper. Ever the sedate female companion, she seems to match her Crane long-legged gait to his casual steps. It is an example of what biologists call "shared behavior."

And it was shared behavior which brought about the most extraordinary story of man and bird, a legendary one akin to Washington Irving's tale of the "Prince Who Speaks the Language of Birds." In Irving's Moorish *Tales of the Alhambra,* is a theme which has run through Arabic literature since the *Koran.*

As a doctoral student, George Archibald learned to decode the "language of Cranes" while writing his dissertation on their "unison call," a work which has enabled scientists to determine Crane gender

Young Cranes sometime need a helping wing.

through their posture and call when paired together. With Tex, Archibald also learned the movement of their dance, the "body-language" of Cranes. It is a knowledge which he has passed on to staff and volunteers exercising a young Brolga Crane in ICF's "chick yard." I have seen a young woman spread her arms like wings and a chick following open-winged and at a run.

The Pedigree of Tex

When Josephine the Louisiana Whooper perished in 1965, as has been mentioned earlier, her spouse Crip and their four progeny survived the results of the Hurricane. Although at that time of mid-sixties, Josephine was the only breeding female Whooper in captivity, there was another captive female Whooper, Rosie, and she resided at the San Antonio Zoo. Rescued from desertion by her mate and her injuries at Aransas, she was taken to San Antonio where she lived a mateless existence.

After they failed to produce offspring by Josephine's and Crip's son, officialdom decided to pair Rosie in San Antonio with Crip a "proven sire." And it worked. The pair mated and produced, after several mishaps, a single viable egg.

The precious egg was taken and incubated by Zoo Director Fred Stark, until at last a wondrous little chick hatched. Fred Stark gave the kind of tender parental care enabling the curious little Whooper to survive. But the chick was a weak creature requiring Stark's absolute attention and care. And although the question of Crane gender was still mysterious (as long as the Crane was alive) s/he was given the name "Tex."

Tex went to live at Patuxent and was ultimately shipped from there to ICF. On April 15, 1975, Ron Sauey picked up Tex at O'Hare Airport. It is Tex's story, which leads us by a labyrinthian route of concern for the survival of an Endangered Bird, that brings us at last to Wisconsin and the ancient dance of Cranes.

Tex, it seems, having first received all human care from Fred Stark in San Antonio then at Patuxent by the biologists, was deeply imprinted on the human male as a caregiver. Thus, it was this "mal-imprinting," done of course to save her life that made Tex susceptible to her deep attachment to humans. And, at ICF, George Archibald was her chosen companion.

The closeness of human and Crane has a long history. The tenth century Chinese poet Lin He-Qing had a Crane companion which would fly over his head and those of his guests as he read them his poetry, enriching his life and his works. In the twentieth century, George Archibald, an ornithologist with the "touch of the poet," lived and worked with his companion Tex. To do so, he moved his office into the field and he learned Crane dancing with her in peak seasonal moments of arousal.

This invitation to the dance went on each breeding season. When Archibald had to absent himself on business, substitutes were sent in. They had to be male humans, for Tex tolerated no females in her sight. Since Tex was distinctly monogamous in her inherent Crane ways, it was George and George alone who could dance with her successfully.

After many artificial inseminations of Tex, season after breeding season with semen shipped from Patuxent, Tex was finally impregnated. The frozen semen packet came from "Killer," a Patuxent Crane whose irascible behavior earned him his heavyweight title. Killer had lived peacefully with a mate for a time, and then, with no apparent aggression as a warning, killed each of two mates outright.

far, far,

the mountain path

is steep

thousands of feet up,

the pass is dangerous

and narrow

on the stone bridge

the moss and

lichen green

from time to time,

a sliver of cloud flying

cascades hang

like skeins of silk

image of the moon

from the deep pool

shining

once more to the top

of Flowering Peak

there waiting still

the coming

of the solitary crane

SHIH TE
(legendary, c. 730)

209

Shady Lane

Ahead of me a sign with a great Red-Crowned Crane flying across an orange sun points the way. I turn right off County Road A, as if urged along by the flying Crane, and I head down Shady Lane Road. Half way between County Road A and busy Highway 12, which leads to the glitzy extravaganza of motels near the natural wonders of the Wisconsin Dells, is ICF. Like an Ojibwa creation story in which Cranes seek and find a perfect place, it is a perfect place for Cranes.

Just across the road from the entrance to ICF another sign rises on its uprights from the farmyard below. On it a larger than life Red-Crowned Crane flies toward the gates as if fueled by the orange sun behind it. In the butterfly light of a Wisconsin fall day I see beneath the signboard a gaggle of Geese conversing in Goose language.

The sign, rising from the neighboring farmyard, is evidence of the ICF's beginnings on the Sauey farm as well as its local concerns within the immediate habitat of Wisconsin farms. But ICF's global reach is there also in the form of the larger-than-life exotic Crane flying towards all the countries of the world where Cranes may be found and where ICF scientists cooperate in field and village with the people of many lands.

The Blue Crane, *Anthropoides paradisea*, also known as the Paradise Crane or Stanley Crane, is the national bird of South Africa and 99% of their population live there. Blue Cranes prefer to feed and nest in dry, grassy uplands instead of wetlands. Like their close relative the Demoiselle Crane, they have head feathers which stand up if agitated or when disturbed. Their habitat has been greatly harmed by deforestation and agricultural encroachment.

Mayday! Mayday! Mayday! 1981

"On May 1, George noticed that Tex was behaving differently. Her food consumption dropped drastically, and she was lethargic....By dawn the next morning Tex had resumed her activities. At noon George palpated her and felt an egg. They built a nest. On May 3 ... at 1:30 in the afternoon [Tex] sat on her nest. George sat next to her and waited. At 3:00 P.M. Tex laid an egg...."

Thus narrates Barbara Katz, nature writer and scientist whose work *So Cranes May Dance* is the source for this chronicle of George and Tex. Katz, who did her field work at ICF, writes with all the good humor and with the same meticulous intensity any one visiting ICF will find in the professional staff and the many volunteer guides.

For Tex finally to lay her egg, it took the same kind of post-laying labor and care that all the pre-nuptial and ritual display took.

"On May 31, the chick pipped," writes Katz. However, it labored on. Not until dusk the next evening did the Whooping Crane chick emerge from inside the dark encapsulation of its egg. The chick was shaky on its little legs as a returning Astronaut snagged from a space capsule and put aboard an aircraft carrier.

But the chick survived and is now a fully mature Whooper residing at ICF. To show their amazement at his incredible arrival, ICF named it with the slang term "Gee Whiz." The first part of his name honored George Gee for his tremendous support from Patuxent. The "Whiz" denoted his whiz-bang and amazing survival.

"Gee Whiz" was born to "Tex" soon after she danced with George Archibald and was artificially inseminated.

Although Gee Whiz now heard bugling over Wisconsin landscape did survive, his mother Tex did not.

While George was away to tell the world the good news of Gee Whiz's presence on earth, Tex was killed. A Raccoon managed to steal inside her pen despite all the protective netting surrounding her.

Far-flung little mammalian carnivore that the Raccoon is, and a survivor itself of hounding, hunting, and trapping since frontier days, one had managed also to kill the first Whooping Crane hatched in captivity. Almost thirty years after a Raccoon killed Rusty in Texas, another Raccoon succeeded in disemboweling the queenly Tex, a fully mature Whooper who had just produced the first Whooping Crane hatched in Wisconsin since they disappeared from their nesting sites of the Midwest. In the later part of the nineteenth century, the last egg of a Whooper was taken from a nest by an egg collector in Iowa.

So Far East of Eden

I park the car beneath shade trees lining the wall along Shady Lane Road. And leaving water for the dog, I cross ICF's circular drive to pass through an interior circle of native wildflowers and tall grasses, the familiar Big Bluestem of my winter home. Here at ICF, Aldo Leopold's land ethic prevails as a motivating force. Native grasses and plants are encouraged to thrive as much as the exotic birds, the Cranes, eleven of the world's fifteen species endangered.

So far east of Eden, yet so near a bird-lover's heaven, there are few other places in the world like the International Crane Foundation. The only comparisons I could possibly draw would be to Vogelpark in Germany and Slimbridge Wild Fowl Trust in England.

Each is a "mecca for bird lovers the world over." And, although each works with government, none is a governmental institution. Each has begun by the work and devotion of private individuals who had a deep reverence for particular families of birds. Each has opened its gates so that the public may witness birds in edenic natural surroundings.

Painting by David Rankin at the International Crane Foundation Headquarters where all of the world's fifteen species of Cranes may be seen.

Gee Whiz!

Entering the visitors center, I pass a knowing receptionist who gives a courteous answer, nodding yes to the question on my first visit: "Will I really be able to see all the world's Cranes?" When I head left, walking beneath trees just turning yellow and a few dry leaves crackling underfoot, I arrive at a large sunny open space grown tall with grasses like a prairie, savannah, or African veld.

There, moving among the grasses, I make out the dark shapes moving in that step-pause-step-step I've grown to recognize as feeding Cranes. One Crane raises its head, and I am startled at its flamboyant yellow crown.

Two pair range through the grasses. Crowned Cranes — the Black-Crowned Crane (*Balearica pavonina*) and the Gray-Crowned Crane (*Balearica regulorum*) — are probably the most extravagant creatures of Cranedom. Their golden crowned heads appear above the grass like a sun's corona. Yet they retain some primitive traits not found in other Cranes. They are nature's exception to the rule. Unlike all the other fifteen species in the world, these Cranes will perch in trees.

Their back toe, the hallux, is not short and elevated like the ground roosting Cranes, but long enough to secure a tree perch. "The presence of this trait" suggests to Paul Johnsgard that Cranes might have evolved from a "perching-adapted ancestor" similar to Limpkins (*Aramus*) and other members of their Order (*Music*).

But I leave off my contemplation of these miraculous creatures, for I hear as if from the summit of my own native wilds, the lordly and triumphant call of a Whooping Crane. I am pulled along as if by its animal magneticism towards the sound.

Topping the hill, I hear it clearly above all the rest of the Cranes conversing in Johnson Pod. Where all the

The Sarus Crane, *Grus antigone*, is the world's tallest flying bird. Males can often stand six feet tall. There are three subspecies: the Indian Sarus Cranes live mostly in northern and central India as well as southeastern Pakistan; Eastern Sarus Cranes were once abundant in Cambodia, Laos, and Viet Nam, but war has ruined much of their range and population; Australian Sarus Cranes are found mostly in the northern part of the continent.

world's Cranes may be seen and heard calling out in their multi-lingual Crane voices, I proceed along a semi-circle of the circular path around the Pod, and zip by whole continents of Crane presence, hurrying past Brolgas of Australia, Wattled Cranes of Africa, Sarus Cranes of India to strike out towards that one dominant call, the Whooping Crane's.

Against the Wisconsin landscape, the distant trees braided with fall color, he stands on a green rise of ground, I see that white gleaming shaped head, uplifted beak pointing to the blue blaze of sky. It is none other than Gee Whiz, rare bird and only son of Tex.

On a first visit to ICF, I wrote down my impressions and after many more visits those impressions haven't changed: to breed all the world's Cranes takes a kind of flexibility found in nature itself. When Bobcat predators killed Whooping Cranes in Florida, Marianne Wellington had to accustom her Florida-bound Cranes to roost in water away from Bobcat danger. When the Siberian Cranes would not produce, the biologists realized that the long daylight of a northern breeding season would have to be imitated. Thus, lights stayed on above the Siberians, and they produced. The same was true of Sarus Cranes, and the rains of India during the breeding system: Thus sprinklers were used to imitate a rainy season, and the Sarus ultimately produced.

The Wattled Crane, *Bugeranus carunculatus*, is primarily found in south-central Africa, but some exist in Ethiopia, South Africa, Namibia, and in the Zambezi Delta on Africa's east coast. No one quite knows why they have "wattles," but when the bird becomes aggressive the wattles stretch larger or else shrink when afraid. Wattled Cranes do not migrate, though they move about searching for better wetlands and foraging territory.

Now, after numerous visits at ICF, I have been able at my leisure to photograph all the world's Cranes and to sit for whole days sketching them as I rounded the world of Cranes — Crane by Crane — in Johnson Pod.

But it has always been the Whooping Cranes which attracted me the most. Once after a three-day festivity in which ICF celebrated its twenty-fifth year of existence, I watched the Whooping Cranes at the Amoco Whooping Crane Exhibit, an architectural wonder of imagination, where Whooping Cranes may be viewed, searching freely for tuber and toad among the marshy reaches as quietly unaware of our presence as they had been before our time.

For the celebration, beginning with the "Eggs Stravaganza," at least three hundred people had come from all over North America and the world, brought together by one single motivating force, their love and fascination for Cranes. Among the world's distinguished visitors, Carl Von Treunfels from Germany was there to give a round-the world Crane slide talk. With him we travelled from the bronze Crane of the China's Forbidden City to the plains of Africa. There he photographed hundreds of Crowned Cranes perched on an enormous tree burgeoning from it like golden crested fruit.

George Archibald.

That night George Archibald announced that the Whooping Crane Recovery Team of which he was a member is in the process of planning the reintroduction of the Whooping Cranes to Wisconsin. They will be led from Wisconsin to Florida by ultralight planes of Operation Migration headed by Bill Lishman. This was the first mention anyone had heard of this plan (it would be, as we have seen earlier, successfully initiated in the fall of 2000.)

The next afternoon I'm again at the Amoco; Gee Whiz and his spouse have been transferred to the privacy of ICF's "Crane City" where the rare Cranes are reared and housed and many are in isolation from humans. A new Crane couple is ensconced in the waterworld.

A few visitors wander in and out. Von Treunfels is deeply occupied with his camera, expertly turning the long-range lens for a good close-up of the Whooping Crane pair. George Archibald leans against a wall; his eyes shielded by a ballcap, he seems to be gazing steadily at a flowering bush.

Watching him, I think after days of celebration, tours, banquets, visiting family, visiting Crane devotees, and officialdom from everywhere, that, even with his enormous reservoir of energy sustaining him on wild Crane research all over the planet, he has to be tired. But I see no evidence of fatigue or stress.

Then I realize why he is gazing so steadily at the flowering bush. A Monarch Butterfly moves from flower to flower. That self-renewing world of nature is his pathway to a deep source. To watch the butterfly, bird, or bush is an act of grace.

A short time after the twenty-fifth celebration of ICF's founding, George Archibald is again on the wing, flying to countries all over the world where Cranes are found. The "common denominator" of his travels "is the Cranes."

After meeting and working with biologists in India at Keolado Reserve where his partner Ron Sauey began the effort to conserve the Siberian Crane, Archibald will go on to the high mountain peaks of Bhutan. Sometimes living in a tent, he will work with the local scientists to put radio transmitters on the rare Black-Necked Crane. Its taxonomy is *Grus nigricollis* but the people call it "Lubja," God's bird.

"The most internationally connected man I know," said the distinguished bird artist Roger Tory Peterson of Archibald. And yet with all the complexities of scientific and governmental connections, clearly he really connects with those moments in nature wherever he is. For one who has been most successful in breeding Cranes in captivity in order to save their precious life forms, what he seems truly to work for is that Cranes will be wild, and they may be free to dance their springtime renewal wherever they are around the world.

International Crane Foundation staff members use a "crane puppet" and spoon to feed baby Cranes.

The Thing with Feathers

A light rain has fallen, and a cool autumn mist is general over Wisconsin and the Great Lakes. After a long fall drought, the Daisy Fleabane, the Compass Plant, and all the other wild flowers and grasses on ICF nature trails surge with a newfound life.

It is late in the day, almost closing time at ICF, so I have the good fortune to be the solitary watcher of the Whooping Crane pair in the marsh.

In the silence, only the reeds talk. The Crane pair feeding on tubers beneath the water step-pause-step in a choreographed and balanced sharing. One of the Cranes stops to preen; a downy feather falls and floats on the surface of the pond moving with even a slight breath of wind. I think of all the hope these birds represent and of the many scientists and birders who gave so much to their survival. "Hope," in the words of poet Emily Dickinson: "is the thing with feathers."

With this attentive silence, I overhear something of what Cranes know — and have known long before my kind stood tall to part the long marsh grass in a wistful and ceaseless search for game.

The pair moves, moves. Their reflections cross, crisscross, join and pair in a composite presence.

I am watching Whooping Cranes move into the silent space inhabited only by the wild stillness of their being.

Afterword

Two Thousand Cranes

In Phoenix, the Arizona city named for the ancient bird resurrected anew from ashes of the old, Thuong Nguyen's "Our World:2000 Paper Cranes" is displayed suspended from the ceiling inside the city library. The exhibit of origami cranes, taking five months to fold and complete, is a spectacular gift to the youth of the city from Nguyen, a Vietnamese artist who escaped the past of his war-torn country when young. Having read of Sadako and her attempt to make a thousand origami Cranes, Thoung says, "I was so deeply moved that I wanted to do 2000 cranes in honor of the new millennium." The *Arizona Republic* headlines the Phoenix exhibit of paper cranes with the words: AN APPEAL FOR PEACE SPREAD ON WINGS OF CRANES!

Also mid-January 2000, in another city of the southwest, Albuquerque, New Mexico, biologists of the North American Crane Working Group and members of the Whooping Crane Conservation Association meet in consecutively planned sessions to confer on the current status of North American Cranes. Like the month of January, named for the double countenanced Roman god Janus, who with one face gazes behind him and with the other looks ahead, the NACWG and the WCCA confer on the past and future welfare of the North American Cranes.

A diverse group of men and women, the Working Group is composed mostly of scientists active in the field. The Conservation Association also has a number of scientists as well as knowledgeable Crane enthusiasts in its membership. In both groups, members come from all over the North American continent. From the steamy savannahs of Florida, from the wetlands of Mississippi, and from the cold zones of Canada and the upper midwest they present their reports, constantly monitoring decreases or increases of Crane populations.

Throughout the Working Group's sessions, one after another scientist, Canadian or US, walks to the podium to present a paper crafted in language honed to a neutral and scientific precision, and amplified by the visuals close to biologists' hearts. Their field observations at the green margins of southern wetlands or in the white snow-covered fields of the northern forests contain within them a clear dedication to Cranes. And, although their charts and graphs are mobilized with data, their

Like a crane
or a swallow
so did
I chatter,
I did mourn
as a dove.
Mine eyes
frail with
looking upward.

ISAIAH
Old Testament

into Autumn dusk

cranes

carry my passion

HAKYO
1913-69

sense of wonder at their encounters with these great birds always seems to take wing.

They have many new technologies to aid their work. New behavioral methods to rear Cranes from the egg so that the birds may sustain and hopefully reproduce life, and vast amounts of data available to them on the World Wide Web enabling them to track wild Cranes. Even the biologist's customary slide talk is now programmed into a computer, the pictures and charts flashed magically upon the screen. But the flexibility to use today's technology and that of the past and of other cultures is epitomized especially by one talk in which Scott Hereford, President of NACWG and the scientist in charge of the endangered subspecies of Sandhill, the Mississippi, presents a "new" gentle way to capture an errant or sick Crane with what he calls a "Clap Trap." This is a form of "rope trick" which is an ancient use of softly coiled rope learned from a villager in India.

One evening of the conference the members of the Whooping Crane Recovery Team established under the Endangered Species Act and chaired by Tom Stehn of the US and Brian Johns of Canada sit around a table to discuss the future plans for all to hear.

Much study of habitat and flyways has gone into the new proposal. But the plan which George Archibald spoke of at ICF's twenty-five year celebration two years ago is to be put into action. A third flock of Whoopers, one in addition to the Texas/Canada migratory flock (now numbering 187) and the Florida resident flock (now with 80 Whoopers) is to be established by drawing on the captive reared Crane populations located at ICF and Patuxent and in various zoos from San Antonio to

Calgary. The hope for the future is that the Cranes will eventually succeed in migrating on their own from Wisconsin to Florida. They fly from the Necedah Wildlife Refuge, Wisconsin to Florida, near the area where William Bartram saw them in the 1700s.

All the accretion of knowledge gained over the past fifty years when the first Whooper was hatched in Texas will be put into play. And behavioral methods and technologies of rearing captive Cranes as well as tracking them in the wild that Robert Porter Allen could only dream of will be used. One method to be used is that Cranes will be "taught" migration routes through imprinting and following ultralight planes to their Florida destination. First the Sandhills will fly behind the ultralights, then the rarer Whoopers will go. The first part of the plan we know now has succeeded. It is a bold and imaginative plan. But it has been the boldness, imagination and hard work of naturalists which have enabled this ancient bird to survive its near extinction in the twentieth century, and as each season passes to spread its wings into new Springs to come.

From the thanka painting "Wheel of Crane Conservation" by Puran shakya for Lumbini Crane Sanctuary, supported by the International Crane Foundation, in Nepal near the birthplace of the Buddha.

Even as a youth, Siddharta possessed a sense of loving-kindness towards all living beings. At times he liked also to go hunting, but so far had never killed the animals he hunted. Instead, he just asked them to play. One day he was out with his cousin Devadatta, who took aim at a Crane and shot it down. The bird fell to the ground half-dead. Siddharta took the Crane in his arms and treated the arrow-wound thereby healing it. Though Devadatta demanded the Crane as his prize, the Buddha said— "A life belongs to those who save it, not to those who take it."

adapted from
The Life of Buddha Gautama
DHYANARAM MAHATHERA

Works Consulted

Abram, David. *The Spell of the Sensuous: Perception and Language in a More-than Human World.* Pantheon Books, 1996.

Adler, Mortimer J., ed. "Biological Treatises of Aristotle." *Great Books of the Western World, Vol. 8.* Encyclopedia Britannica, Inc., 1991.

_____. "The History of Herodotus." *Great Books of the Western World, Vol. 5.* Encyclopedia Britannica, Inc., 1991.

Aldington, Richard and Delano Ames, trans. *New La Rousse Encyclopedia of Mythology.* Hamlin Publishing, 1970.

Allen, Robert Porter. *On the Trail of Vanishing Birds.* McGraw-Hill Book Co., Inc., 1957.

_____. *The Whooping Crane: Research Report No. 3.* Audubon Society, 1952.

Allen, Thomas B., ed. *Marvels of Animal Behavior.* National Geographic Society, 1972.

Anesaki, Masaharu. *Japan, Vol. III. Mythology of All Races.* Archaeological Institute of America, 1928.

Archibald, George. "Introduction." *Marshland Elegy* by Aldo Leopold. Wisconsin Center for the Book, Wisconsin Academy of Sciences, Arts and Letters, 1999.

Archibald, George and Jim Lewis. "Learning to Migrate." *The ICF Bugle, Vol. 22, No. 4 ICF,* 1996.

Armstrong, Edward A. "The Crane Dance in East and West." *Antiquity,* 1973.

Asch, Connie. *Indian Designs.* Treasure Chest Publications, 1985.

Atkinson, M. Jourdan. *Indians of the Southwest.* The Naylor Co., 1955.

Attenborough, David. *The Life of Birds.* Princeton University Press, 1998.

Audubon, John James. *The Complete Audubon, Vol. III, Birds of America* (facsimile of 1842 edition). Volaire Ltd., 1979.

Bailey, Florence Merriam. *The Birds of New Mexico.* New Mexico Department of Game and Fish, 1939.

Barnett, Martha. *A Garden of Words.* Times Books, 1992.

Bauval, Robert and Graham Hancock. *The Message of the Sphinx.* Three Rivers Press, 1996.

Bent, Arthur Cleveland. *Life Histories of North American Marsh Birds.* Republished by Dover Press, 1963.

Benton-Banai, Edward. *The Mishomis Book: The Voice of the Ojibway.* Indian Country Communications, 1988.

Berlandier, Jean Luois. *Journey to Mexico, Vol. II.* Texas State Historical Society and University of Texas, 1980.

Berry, Wendell. *Traveling at Home.* North Point Press, 1989.

Beyer, Nelson, Sabra Niebur, and Anna Morton. "Importance of Genetic Diversity in Whooping Cranes." *Patuxent Science Notes.* Patuxent Wildlife Research Center, 1996.

Biederman, Hans. *Dictionary of Symbolism.* Penguin Group, 1994.

Bizeau, Elliott G. "The Whooping Crane Transplant." Appendix in *The Whooping Crane* by Jerome J. Pratt. Castle Rock Publishers, 1996.

Blaau, F.E. *A Monograph of the Cranes.* Leyden/London, 1897.

Blyth, Edward. Revised and edited by W.B. Tegetmeier, *The Natural History of Cranes*, Horace Cox, 1881.

Branston, Brian. *The Lost Gods of England*. Oxford University Press, 1974.

Britton, D. and T. Hayashida. *The Japanese Crane: Bird of Happiness*. Kodansha International, 1993.

Brooke, Michael and Tim Birkhead, eds. *The Cambridge Encyclopedia of Ornithology*. Cambridge University Press, 1991.

Bull, John and John Farrand, Jr. *The Audubon Society Field Guide to North American Birds: Eastern Region*. Alfred A. Knopf, Inc., 1977.

Campbell, Joseph. *The Power of Myth*. Doubleday, 1988.

Capra, Fritjof. "The Emerging New Culture." *Thinking Allowed*. Council Oaks Books, 1992.

_____. *The Web of Life: A New Scientific Understanding*. Anchor Books, 1996.

Castleden, Rodney. World History: A Chronological Dictionary of Dates. Paragon, 1998.

Catesby, Mark. *The Natural History of Carolina, Florida, and the Bahamas*. "Printed at the expense of the Author," 1731.

Chronic, Halka. *Roadside Geology of New Mexico*. Mountain Press Publishing Company, 1987.

Clauss, Brian. "Maryland Cranes Fly to the Aid of the Whooper." *American Pheasant and Waterfowl Magazine*, November, 1996.

Clocksin, W.F. "Knowledge, Representation and Myth." *Nature's Imagination: The Frontiers of Scientific Vision*. Oxford University Press, 1995.

Cory, Charles B. *The Birds of Illinois and Wisconsin*. Field Museum of Chicago, 1909.

Coues, Elliott. *Key to North American Birds: General Ornithology and Field Ornithology*. Estes and Lauriat, 1890.

Cushing, Frank Hamilton. *Zuni: Selected Writings of Frank Hamilton Cushing*. Edited by Jesse Green. University of Nebraska, 1979.

Cypher, John. *Bob Kleberg and The King Ranch: A Worldwide Sea of Grass*. University of Texas Press, 1995.

Doughty, Robin W. *Return of the Whooping Crane*. University of Texas Press, 1989.

Drewien, Roderick. "Seasonal Movements of Sandhill Cranes Radiomarked in Yellowstone National Park and Jackson Hole, Wyoming." *Journal of Wildlife Management*, 1999.

Dudley, Carol. *Whooping Cranes: The Untamed World*. Weigl Educational Publishers, Ltd., 1997.

Dysler, David D., producer and screenwriter. *Flight of the Whooping Crane*. National Geographic Society and WQED, 1984.

Dyson, Freeman. "The Scientist as Rebel." *Nature's Imagination: The Frontiers of Scientific Vision*. Oxford University Press, 1995.

Ehrlich, Paul and Anne Ehrlich. *Extinction: The Causes and Consequences of the Disappearance of the Species*. Random House, 1981.

Eisley, Loren. *The Invisible Pyramid*. Charles Scribner's Sons, 1970.

Eliot, Alexander. *The Universal Myths*. Meridian Books, 1990.

Ellis, David H., George F. Gee, Claire M. Mirande, eds. *Cranes: Their Biology, Husbandry, and Conservation*. Department of Interior, National Biological Service, and The International Crane Foundation, 1996.

Farber, Paul Lawrence. *Discovering Birds: The Emergence of Ornithology as a Scientific Discipline, 1760-1850*. Johns Hopkins University Press, 1997.

Ferguson, Reverend George. *Signs and Symbols of Christian Art*. Oxford University Press, c.1954.

Forbush, Edward Howe in *Birds of America*. Edited by Gilbert T. Pason. Garden City Books, 1936.

Franciscan Fathers, eds. *An Ethnologic Dictionary*. Franciscan Fathers, 1910.

Friedman, Judy. *Operation Siberian Crane: The Story Behind the Effort to Save an Amazing Bird*. Dillion Press, 1995.

Frisbie, Theodore R. "Southwestern Indians and Cranes." *The ICF Bugle, Vol. 12, No. 1*, February, 1986.

Garbarino, Merwyn S. *The Seminole*. Chelsea House Publishers, 1989.

Garrett, Wilbur E., ed. "The Southwest: The Making of America." *Cartographic Division of National Geographic*, 1982.

Gernsheim, Helmut and Alison Gernsheim. "Rediscovery of the World's First Photograph." *The Photographic Journal*, May, 1952.

Gimbutas, Marija, *The Goddesses and Gods of Old Europe: Myths and Cult Images*. University of California Press, 1992.

Gomez, Gay M. "Whooping Cranes in Southwest Louisiana: History and Human Attitudes." *Proceedings North American Crane Workshop*. North American Crane Working Group, 1992.

Graham, Frank, Jr. with Carl Buchheister. *The Audubon Ark: A History of the National Audubon Society*. Alfred A. Knopf, 1990.

Grant, Campbell. *Rock Art of the American Indian*. Thomas Y. Crowell Co., 1967.

Grant, Michael, ed. *The Birth of Western Civilization: Greece and Rome*. McGraw-Hill Co., 1964.

Graves, Robert. *The Greek Myths*. Moyer Bell, Ltd., 1960.

_____. *The White Goddess: A Historical Grammar of Poetic Myth*. Farrar, Straus and Giroux, 1970.

Green, Miranda. *The Gods of the Celts*. Sutton Publishing, 1997.

Greenwald, Jeff. "Who's Out There?" *Discover*, April, 1999.

Griswold, John A. *Proven Methods of Keeping and Rearing Cranes in Captivity*. International Waterfowl Association, 1962.

Grooms, Steve. *The Cry of the Sandhill Crane*. Northward Press, 1992.

Hallam, Anthony, ed. *Encyclopedia of Planet Earth*. Exeter Books, 1997.

Harding, Terri, ed. "Ojibway." *Legends and Lore of the North American Indians*. Barnes and Noble, 1993.

Harman, Willis. *Global Mind Change: The Promise of the Twenty-First Century*. Berrett-Koehler Publishers, Inc., 1998.

Harper, Francis, ed. *The Travels of William Bartram*. Naturalist's Edition. University of Georgia Press, 1998.

Harriot, Thomas. *A Briefe and True Report of the New Found Land of Virginia (1590 DeBry Edition)*. Dover Books, 1972.

Harris, Jim. "Six Countries Join North East Asian Crane Network." *The ICF Bugle Vol. 24, no. 4*, November 1998.

Harrison, Thomas P., ed. *The First Watercolors of North American Birds*. Univeristy of Texas Press, c.1950s.

Harrison, Thomas P. and F. David Hoeniger, eds. *The Fowles of Heaven, or History of Birds by Edward Topsell*. University of Texas Press, 1972.

Higgins, Reynold. *Minoan and Mycenaean Art*. Thames and Hudson, 1981.

Hoagland, Kathleen. *One Thousand Years of Irish Poetry*. Devin-Adair Co., 1955.

Hogben, Lancelot. *The Vocabulary of Science*. Stein and Day Publishers, 1970.

Houlihan, Patrick F. *The Birds of Ancient Egypt*. Aris and Phillips, 1986.

Hulton, Paul, ed. *The Complete Drawings of John White*. University of North Carolina Press and British Museum Publications, 1984.

_____. "Introduction" to *A Briefe And True Report of the New Found Land of Virginia by Thomas Harriott (1590)*, Dover, 1972.

Ingersoll, Ernest. *Birds in Legend, Fable and Folklore*. Longmans, Green and Company, 1923.

International Crane Foundation. "The Whooping Crane: Symbol of International Cooperation." ICF, 1998.

Johnsgard, Paul A. *Crane Music: A Natural History of American Cranes*. Smithsonian Institution Press, 1991.

_____. *Cranes of the World*. Indiana University Press, 1983.

_____. *Those of the Gray Wind*. University of Nebraska Press, 1986.

Kacian, Jim. *Six Directions: Haiku*. La Alameda Press, 1997.

Kastner, Joseph. *A Species of Eternity*. Alfred A. Knopf, Inc., 1977.

Katz, Barbara. *So Cranes May Dance*. Chicago Review Press, Inc., 1993.

Kerenyi, C. *The Gods of the Greeks*. Book Collectors Society, 1950.

Kingery, Donna. Unpublished letter, 1997.

Kingery, Tanner. "Hazardous Powerlines: A Crane/Powerline Study." Unpublished, 1984.

Kowalski, Gary. *The Souls of Animals*. Stillpoint Publishing, 1991.

Kluckholm, Clyde, W.W. Hill, and Lucy Wales Kluckholm. *Navaho Cultural Material*. Belknap Press of Harvard University Press, 1971.

Kumlien, L. and N. Hollister. "The Birds of Wisconsin." *Bulletin of Wisconsin Natural History Society*, 1903.

Langhorne, John and William Langhorne, eds. and trans. *Plutarch's Lives*. Derby and Jackson, 1859.

Lavitt, Edward and Robert E. McDowell, eds. *Nihuacans' Feast of Beaver: Animal Tales of the North American Indian*. Museum of New Mexico Press, 1990.

Leitch, Barbara A. *A Concise Dictionary of Indian Names of North America*. Reference Publications Inc., 1979.

Leopold, Aldo. *A Sand County Almanac*. Oxford University Press, 1949.

Levi-Strauss, Claude. *Myth and Meaning: Cracking the Code of Culture*. University of Toronto Press, 1978.

Lewis, James. "P-R-O-G-R-E-S-S in Recovering the Whooping Crane." *Bosque del Apache Habitat*. Friends of the Bosque del Apache NWR, Inc., Vol. 4, No. 1, 1997.

Lorenz, Konrad. *Here I Am — Where Are You? The Behavior of the Greylag Goose*. Harcourt Brace Jovanovich, 1992.

Maddox, John (Sir). *What Remains to Be Discovered*. The Free Press, 1998.

Mallery, Garrick. *Picture-Writing of the Amiercan Indians*. *Vols. 1 and 2*, first published 1893, republished by Dover Press, 1972.

Marquez, Gabriel Garcia. *Chronicle of a Death Foretold*. Translated by Gregory Rabassa. Alfred A. Knopf, 1982.

Maurer, Stephen G. *Bosque del Apache National Wildlife Refuge*. Southwest Natural and Cultural Heritage Association, 1994.

Mayr, Ernst. *This is Biology: The Science of the Living World*. Belknap Press of Harvard
        University, 1997.

McManus, Seumas. *The Story of the Irish Race*. Devin-Adair Company, 1974.

McNulty, Faith. *The Whooping Crane: The Bird That Defies Extinction*. Clarke, Irwin, and
        Company, Ltd., 1996.

McPhee, John. "The Gravel Page," *New Yorker*, January 29, 1996.

Meine, Curt D. and George W. Archibald, eds. *The Cranes: Status Survey and Conservation Plan*.
        IUCN, Switzerland and United Kingdom, 1996.

National Science Foundation. *The Very Large Array*, 1989.

Nesbitt, Stephen A. and Clinton T. Moore and Kathleen S. Williams. "Gender Prediction from
        Body Measurements of Two Subspecies of Sandhill Cranes." *Proceedings of the North
        American Crane Workshop*, North American Crane Working Group, 1991.

New York, *City of. American Wildlife Illustrated*. William H. Wise and Company, Inc., 1954.

Nixon, Jay. *Stewards of a Vision: A History of the King Ranch*. King Ranch, Inc., 1986.

Ortiz, Alfonso. *The Tewa World: Space, Time, Being and Becoming in a Pueblo Society*. University
        of Chicago Press, 1969.

Parsons, Elsie Clews, ed. *American Indian Life*. B.W. Huebsch, Inc.,1922.

Patent, Dorothy Hinshaw. *The Whooping Crane: A Comeback Story*. Clarion Books, 1988.

Peattie, Donald Culcross. *Green Laurels: The Lives and Achievements of the Great Naturalists*.
        Simon and Schuster, Inc., 1936.

Pratt, Jerome J., ed. *Whooping Crane Conservation Association Newsletter*, Spring, 1998.
        _____. *The Whooping Crane: North America's Symbol of Conservation*. Castle Rock
        Publishing Company, 1996.

Preston, J.W. "My First White Crane's Nest." *The Oologist, Vol.4, No. 4*, July & August, 1886.

Price, A(lice) Lindsay. *Swans of the World: In Nature, History, Myth and Art*. Council Oak
        Books, 1994.

Proctor, Noble S. and Patrick J. Lynch. *Manual of Ornithology: Avian Structure and Function*. Yale
        University Press, 1993.

Robbins, Samuel D., Jr. *Wisconsin Birdlife: Population and Distribution Past and Present*.
        The University of Wisconsin Press, 1991.

Rogers, Phillip M. and Donald A. Hammer. "Ancestral Breeding and Wintering Ranges of
        the Trumpeter Swan in the Eastern United States." *Swans: Bulletin of the Trumpeter
        Swan Society*, December, 1998.

Rothenberg, Jerome. *Technicians of the Sacred: A range of Poetries from Africa, America, Asia,
        Europe & Oceania*. University of California Press, 1985.

Rozinski, Robert, Wendy Shattil, and Virginia McConnell Simmons. *Valley of the Cranes:
        Exploring Colorado's San Luis Valley*. Roberts Rinehart, Inc., Publishers, 1988.

Schleussner, Gunther. "Germany's Vogelpark Walsrode." *Game Bird Breeders and Conservationists
        Gazette*, November, 1994.

Schoff, Gretchen Holstein. *Reflections: The Story of Cranes*. International Crane Foundation, 1991.

Scott, Dorothea Hayward. *A Flight of Cranes: Stories and Poems from Around the World*.
        The Denvil Press, 1990.

Scott, Peter. *Observations of Wildlife*. Phaidon Press, 1980.

Seaton, J.P. and Maloney, Dennis. *A Drifting Boat: Chinese Zen Poetry*. White Pine Press, 1994.

Seton, Ernest Thompson. *Lives of the Hunted*. Charles Scribners, 1905.
_____. *On the Trail of an Artist-Naturalist*. Scribners, 1940.
Slaughter, Thomas P. *The Natures of John and William Bartram*. Random House, Inc., 1997.
Smirnova, Galina. *Fairy Tales of Siberian Folks*. Krasnoyarsk "Vital" Publishers, 1992.
Socorro, *City of. Socorro County Guidebook*. Socorro Local Merchants and Community of
        Socorro, 1997.
Spyropoulos, Spyros and Eugene Vanderpool. *Birds of the Athenian Agora*. American School
        of Classical Studies at Athens, 1985.
Sprunt, Alexander, Jr. *Florida Bird Life*. Based on a supplement to *Florida Bird Life* by
        Arthur H. Howell published in 1932. Coward-McCann, National Audubon Society,
        and U.S. Fish and Wildlife Service, 1954.
Stafford, William. "Watching Sandhill Cranes." *Even in Quiet Places*. Confluence Press, 1996.
Stahlecker, Dale and Martin Frentzel. *Seasons of the Crane*. Heritage Associates, Inc., 1986.
Stanley, Edward Smith. *A Familiar History of Birds*. Longmans and Company, c.1850s.
Steffurud, Alfred, ed. *Birds in Our Lives*. Arco Publishing Company, 1970.
Sullivan, Walter. *Landprints on the Magnificent American Landscape*. Time Books, 1984.
Symons, R.D. *Hours and the Birds: A Saskatchewan Record*. Canada, 1967.

Tattersall, Ian. *The Human Odyssey*. Prentice Hall General Reference, 1993.
Taverner, P.A. *Birds of Eastern Canada. No. 3*, Biological Series, F.A. Acland, 1922.
Thomas, Alfred Barnaby, ed. and trans. *Forgotten Frontiers: A Study of the Spanish Indian Policy of
        Don Juan Bautista de Anza, Gov. of New Mexico 1777-1787*. University of Oklahoma
        Press, 1932.
Thoreau, Henry David. "Journals of Henry David Thoreau." *The Norton Book of Nature Writing*,
        W.W. Norton, 1990.
Treuenfels, Carl-Albert V. *Kraniche: Vogel des Glücks*. Rash und Rohring, 1996.
Tyler, Hamilton A. *Pueblo Birds and Myths*. Northland Publishing, 1991.

U.S. Fish and Wildlife Service. "The Whooping Crane: An Endangered Species." *USFWS*, 1990.

Waldman, Carl. *Timelines of Native American History*. Prentice Hall General Reference, 1995.
Walker, James R. *Lakota Myth*. University of Nebraska Press, 1983.
Walkinshaw, Lawrence. *Cranes of the World*. Winchester Press, 1973.
_____. *The Sandhill Cranes. Bulletin no. 29*, Cranbrook Institute of Science, 1949.
Waterman, Talbot H. *Animal Navigation*. Scientific American Books, Inc., 1989.
Weitzman, Martin L. "What To Preserve? An Application of Diversity Theory to Crane Conservation." The
        Quarterly Journal of Economics, February, 1993.
Wells, Lawrence. "The Old Man and the Keys." *Southwest Airlines Spirit*, March 1999.
Whitaker, Barbara. "At the King Ranch, A Way of Life is Riding into the Sunset." *New York Times*,
        Sunday, June 6, 1996.
Wilbur, Ken. *The Marriage of Sense and Soul: Integrating Science and Religion*. Random House,1998
Williams, Terry Tempest. *Refuge*. Pantheon, 1991.
Wilson, Alexander and Charles Lucien Bonaparte. *American Ornithology: Natural History of the Birds of
        the United States*. Porter and Coates, 1831.
Wilson, Edward O. "Biodiversity Threatened." *American Nature Writings*, Sierra Club Books, 1995.
_____. *Consilience: The Unity of Knowledge*. Vintage Books, 1999.
_____. "Introduction" to *Witness: Endangered Species of North America*. California Academy
        of Sciences/ Middleton/Littschwager, 1994.

Sources for Further Crane Information

INTERNATIONAL CRANE FOUNDATION
E-11376 Shady Lane Road, P.O. Box 447, Baraboo, Wisconsin 53913 (608) 356-9462
World center for the study and preservation of Cranes.
They have a great website: www.savingcranes.org — with in-depth information about every species of Crane, environmental education resources, conservation, and links to other organizations and research source material. They publish a wonderful newsletter — *The Bugle.*

WHOOPING CRANE CONSERVATION ASSOCIATION
1393 Henderson Highway, Breaux Bridge, Louisiana 70517
www.whoopingcrane.com
Up-to-date information of Whooping Cranes in their newsletter.

NORTH AMERICAN CRANE WORKING GROUP
341 W. Olympic Place, Seattle, Washington 98119
www.portup.com/~nacwg/ — excellent links to other organizations
They publish a fine newsletter — *The Unison Call.*

THE GREEN LANE / ENVIRONMENT CANADA / PRAIRIE & NORTHERN REGION WHOOPING CRANE
www.mb.ec.gc.ca/index/.en
Information about Canadian migration patterns and Wood Buffalo National Park.

NATIONAL AUDUBON SOCIETY
700 Broadway, New York City, New York 10003 (212) 979-3000
www.audubon.org
"The mission is to conserve and restore natural ecosystems, focusing on birds and other wildlife for the benefit of humanity and the earth's biological diversity."

BOSQUE DEL APACHE NATIONAL WILDLIFE REFUGE
P.O. Box 1246, Socorro, New Mexico 87801 (505) 835-1828
www.southwest.fws.gov/refuges/newmex/bosque
They host a "Festival of Cranes" every November.

LILLIAN ANNETTE ROWE SANCTUARY
44450 Elm Island Road, Gibbon, Nebraska 68840 (308) 469-5282
www.rowesanctuary.org
They offer special guided field trips to view the world's largest concentration of Cranes from observation blinds on the banks of the Platte River.

ARANSAS NATIONAL WILDLIFE REFUGE
P.O. Box 100, Austwell, Texas 77950 (361) 286-3559
www.southwest.fwsgov/refuges/texas/aransas

PATUXENT WILDLIFE REARCH CENTER OF THE US GEOLOGICAL SURVEY
12100 Beech Forest Road, Suite 4039 Laurel, Maryland 20708   (301) 497-5500
www.pwrc.nbs.gov

MISSISSIPPI SANDHILL CRANE WILDLIFE REFUGE
7200 Crane Lane, Gautier, Mississippi 39553   (228) 497-6322

BERNARD W. BAKER SANCTUARY
21145 15 Mile Road, Bellevue, Michigan 49021
www.michiganaudubon.org/bakersanctuary
They host an annual "Crane Fest."

WHOOPING CRANE EASTERN PARTNERSHIP
www.bringbackthecranes.org
A good site for links about the effort to reintroduce a migratory flock to the Eastern United States.

OPERATION MIGRATION
P.O. Box 868, Buffalo, New York 14207   (800) 675-2618
www.operationmigration.org
They have a great website with fabulous photographs taken in the air alongside Cranes!

ALDO LEOPOLD FOUNDATION, INC.
P.O. Box 77, Baraboo, Wisconsin 53913   (608) 355-0279
www.aldoleopold.org —a website chockful of Aldo Leopold lore and resources.
"That land is a community is the basic concept of ecology, but that land is to be loved and respected in an extension of ethics."

DUCKS UNLIMITED
One Waterfowl Way, Memphis, Tennessee 38120   (800-45DUCKS)
www.ducks.org (also many of the chapters in various states have their own websites)
"To fulfill the annual life cycle needs of North American waterfowl by protecting, enhancing, restoring, and managing important wetlands and associated uplands."

NATIONAL FISH AND WILDLIFE FOUNDATION
1120 Connecticut Ave. Suite 900, Washington, D.C. 20036   (202-857-0166)
www.nfwf.org
Set up by Congress, they award funds to projects benefitting conservation, education, habitat protection and restoration, and natural resource management.

MAJESTIC & ENDANGERED WHOOPING CRANES
http://raysweb.net/specialplaces/pages/crane.html
A compilation of Whooping Crane links to a wide range of organizations and articles. Information galore.

THOUSAND CRANES PEACE NETWORK
www.rosella.apana.org.au/~mlb/cranes/index
A site with both information about Cranes/Crane symbology and the use of folded paper Cranes to help promote peace, non-violence, and tolerance in the world. Many interesting links.

INDEX

COLOPHON

Set in *Garamond 3*, one of the typefaces named after
Claude Garamond, who established the first type foundry
in France in the 16th century. Various arguments range
concerning the actual punch-cutter who designed
the original face—Robert Granjon, Garamond's pupil
or Jean Jannon, a Parisian printer whose specimen
was ultimately adopted by Cardinal Richelieu for
the French National Printing Office in 1640.
This version, Garamond 3, was introduced by the
American Type Founders and based on a cutting
by Morris Benton in 1919 which follows the design
of the Jannon letter. As typical of Benton's revivals,
the concern was to keep the classic Old Style
while furthering the needs of mechanical
reproduction in his time. Fortunately,
its graceful and lively form
remains in its usefulness
as a book face.

Titling in Bernhard Modern.

•

Book design by J.B. Bryan

ALICE LINDSAY PRICE
is a nature writer, photographer, poet, artist.
Her most recent book is
Swans of the World:
In Nature, History, Myth & Art
(Council Oak Books, 1994).
She lives in Tulsa, Oklahoma.